In a Class of Your Own:
Managi...

Also available from Continuum:

Getting the Buggers to Behave 3rd Edition – Sue Cowley

Managing your Classroom 2nd Edition – Gererd Dixie

Other titles in the behaviour management series:
Dos & Don'ts of Behaviour Management – Roger Dunn

Managing Behaviour in the Early Years – Janet Kay

Managing Boys' Behaviour – Tabatha Rayment

Managing Very Challenging Behaviour – Louisa Leaman

In a Class of Your Own: Managing Pupils' Behaviour

Bill Gribble

continuum

Dedicated to my wife, Colette, because she is simply the best!

Continuum International Publishing Group

The Tower Building	80 Maiden Lane
11 York Road	Suite 704
London	New York
SE1 7NX	NY 10038

www.continuumbooks.com

© Bill Gribble 2006
billgribble@btinternet.com

British Library Cataloguing-in-Publication Data
A catalogue record for this book is available from the British Library.

ISBN 0–8264–8553–7 (paperback)

Library of Congress Cataloging-in-Publication Data
A catalog record for this book is available from the Library of Congress.

Typeset by BC Typesetting Ltd, Bristol BS31 1NZ
Printed and bound in Great Britain by
Antony Rowe Ltd, Chippenham, Wiltshire

Contents

Contents

Contents

Foreword

Any book that addresses the complex issues of behaviour management in schools today takes on a challenging task. Bill Gribble, the author of this book, is more than familiar with the wide range of issues teachers and support staff face, from the daily irritations of attentional behaviour through to challenging and socio-emotional behaviour difficulties (SEBDs). Bill has had wide experience in SEBD as well as being a consultant advising many schools in the other areas addressed in this book: teaching styles, student disaffection, evaluating and monitoring behaviours, effective management and discipline, meaningful pedagogy, whole-school approaches and colleague support.

He knows schools and students and is clearly sensitive to the stresses we all face in our profession day to day. This book has a strong emphasis on collegiality and whole-school support. The book's title is 'In a Class *of* Your Own' not 'In a Class *on* Your Own' and Bill is able to show us how to invite and give colleague support as we seek to lead and teach young people with confidence and dignity.

Foreword

This book is clearly based in knowledgeable practice (in pedagogy and discipline); it is also practical, sensible and accessible. It is encouraging to see such a wide range of issues addressed with candour, sensitivity and good humour. This book will enable, encourage and support individual and collegial reflection in the critical area of pupil behaviour.

Dr Bill Rogers
Adjunct Professor of Education, Griffith University
Australia

Preface

This collection of thoughts and ideas would not have been possible without the inspiration of Dr Bill Rogers and many other friends and colleagues.

In a Class of Your Own is written for staff in schools to assist them in their management of and planning for pupil behaviour. It is also written for the thousands of teachers with whom I have worked over many years as teacher, headteacher, adviser and consultant. Their wealth of experience and kind comments have made me very optimistic for the future of the profession.

I am especially grateful to the teacher who said to me when I was pointing out the danger of group sanctions that he felt that they were justified on some occasions. In debating this with him he told me that he was working with very behaviourally challenging pupils as a head of year. After surviving a particularly difficult lesson with a Year 10 class, he decided to give the whole class a detention. I said to him that this was a questionable course of action as he could have alienated the pupils who had not misbehaved. He agreed, but said he knew that if he gave a detention then only the 'good' kids would turn up. I asked him if he felt that this was counter-productive. 'On the contrary,' he said, 'all the pupils who turned up for the detention were rewarded with a bottle of Coke and a chocolate bar, thanked for coming and sent away.' I asked him what that had achieved. He said, 'The other pupils heard what had transpired and those who had been involved in minor disruptions came the next day for detention. They received a warning and a packet of crisps!' On the third day, the 'hardcore' of four difficult pupils came for their detention. After half an hour of completing the work that should have been completed previously, one of the group said 'Where's our crisps and drink?' The head of year said, 'Come on, you're three days late for your detention, what do you expect!'

It is teachers like him that make the job so enjoyable. He had made his point to the pupils in a non-confrontational manner and achieved his outcome of getting the work completed. He has also shown me that there is always another way of doing things. I believe that there are a few principles in the management of pupil behaviour, which I hope I have included in the following pages. However, we will always need a range of different strategies to manage classroom behaviour effectively, and colleagues who sometimes reflect upon situations differently from us. Together, I hope we will make a difference and enrich the educational experience for pupils in schools.

Bill Gribble
July 2005

Introduction

This book will consider behaviours that enhance or detract from the teaching and learning process. This consideration will include teacher behaviour as well as pupil behaviour.

This is a book that could have been written by any adult in a school context. We all teach behaviour. It is the type of book I wished I had access to when I first started out in the teaching profession. I hope this collection of ideas helps all teachers. I am indebted to everyone who brought me to this level of understanding, through their patience, consideration and selfless dedication to the craft of pedagogy.

Aim

The aim of this book is to present ideas that help teachers and their colleagues in schools to manage behaviour and to improve the process of teaching and learning. The ideas presented will not comprise a definitive list; there are no 'right' or 'wrong' answers or panaceas.

1

Objectives

This book will concentrate on four interrelated objectives in an attempt to meet its aim. The first:

To understand pupils' behaviour and the influence upon that behaviour by the adults who work with them.

The focus of this objective will be on behaviour exhibited in classroom and school situations. There will be a consideration of the range of adults in the context of the school who, through their behaviour, give messages to pupils about what is acceptable or unacceptable behaviour. Can we gain respect from pupils if there are adults in this context who, as the significant, influential authority figures, employ disrespectful working practices in their dealings with colleagues and pupils?

The second objective:

To develop a planned response to behaviour in class-room and school situations that enhances the process of teaching and learning.

Planning of this type, through an analysis of both adult and pupil behaviour in classrooms and schools, will result in strategies to address behaviour that impedes teaching and learning. Such strategies can be developed from current tried-and-tested, school-based, effective, adult behaviour. These are planned responses, cor-porately understood in advance of the need to employ them. It is hoped that the planning process, when undertaken by adults, will assist them in understanding the emotions that drive their behaviours as well as their pupils' behaviour. The strategies developed will assist in maintaining the flow of the lesson and in turn increase teaching and learning time for all pupils in the class-room setting.

This analysis and planning for responses to behaviour by adults in the school context will, it is hoped, assist in reaching the third objective:

To attempt to make teaching and learning a more positive experience for everyone in a school context.

That is, for both pupils and adults alike. This will be an attempt to develop the basis of a mutually agreed set of working practices or rules for pupils and adults that will assist and enhance the process of teaching and learning.

The final objective of this book in meeting its aim will be:

To assist adults working with pupils in school to reflect upon their working practices in an attempt to develop and add to their range of skills.

The consequence of this self-analysis is to assist adults in gathering evidence upon which to develop their behavioural strategies in the classroom and school. Ideally, the outcome of such self-analysis should be an opportunity to share successful strategies in the development of a collegiate, whole-school approach.

Teachers of behaviour

A teacher of behaviour is defined, for the purposes of this book, as any adult who comes into contact with pupils in a school context. In my opinion, all adults in schools teach pupils acceptable and unacceptable behaviour through their actions and interactions with them. Most behaviour is learned in the early, formative years from the adults and peers. With this knowledge, it is my thesis that we can plan for behaviour in a similar way to the way we plan for curriculum delivery. This is not always realized, recognized or understood by the participants in the process of education at school. However, the impact of adult behaviour on teaching and learning in school is critical for the pupil in terms of inclusion, or exclusion, from the process of education. Therefore, this book will consider the importance of adult/teacher behavioural self-control in a school context. The book will look to assist teachers in developing acceptable behaviours in themselves as well as in children and young people. These are behaviours that will assist pupils in successfully accessing teaching and learning in a school and classroom context.

As a teacher, I know that teaching is one of the most important professions in society. Well-considered teaching provides the correct curriculum diet for society's needs. This is the educational process. This process helps pass on a society's current, collective knowledge to its children. In turn, the process builds society's knowledge base; children can learn and, ideally, develop new knowledge. These functions help perpetuate and develop a healthy society. However, if the process excludes access to education, for whatever reason, it may fail to meet the needs, both real and perceived, of a number of parents and pupils. The resulting behaviour is currently termed in the UK as 'disaffection' or 'disengagement'.

As I write, pupil and parent disaffection in the education system is of increasing concern to many of those involved in the day-to-day running and development of schools in the UK. Thus, the term 'disengagement' has entered our behavioural vocabulary. It is of great concern that elements of society are becoming disengaged through their non-attendance and/or exclusion from the education process. Disengagement can be either active or passive and will be considered in the following pages.

Historically, the education system in the UK has evolved from the education of the privileged few to the education of all. This process now encompasses the right of access to education in the early years and the concept of 'lifelong learning' as a societal responsibility. This rapid and continual evolution of the British education system has meant that many practitioners in schools have also become disengaged as they struggle to assimilate change. Lord Elton in the Elton Report (1989) suggested that:

'Teachers are not beaten up but they are beaten down.'

As I write, I wonder what has changed? There are many practitioners in our schools who feel very much 'beaten down' by the number of new initiatives issued by central government that they are expected to assimilate into their working practices. I suggest in this book that disengagement is both a societal as well as an educational phenomenon. For the adults involved in delivering education, I believe, their disaffection and fears of disengagement can be allayed by empathetic access to training and observation opportunities, as an aspect of their personal and professional development.

The educator has difficulty in addressing all of society's ills, although they are often employed by government as society's scapegoat. With constructive direction and vision, educators could begin to address those difficulties in a given context: the school. I strongly believe, both from personal experiences and involvement in the educational process, that disaffection in and disengagement from school, in all its manifestations, can be addressed and overcome for the vast majority of pupils and practitioners.

There will, however, always be a small and currently growing minority of pupils whose social, emotional and behavioural development will have greater priority than their academic achievement. Their priority must not be allowed to detract from other pupils' educational achievements. The challenge, evident in UK schools, is how to balance the growing priority of social, emotional and behavioural development with academic achievement. An understanding, or lack of understanding, by the adults who work in school where that school's pupil population is at in terms of its emotional and behavioural development will, I feel, lead to its future success or failure.

A key to this success appears increasingly to be encompassed in the pedagogical style promoted by the school.

Pedagogy encompasses the instruction, discipline and training system promoted by a school, and can either engage or disengage the learner. Accordingly, the behaviour of the pedagogue, the adult who promotes the pedagogy, is integral to this process. Their aim: to engage the learner in formal education at school, or as Dr Brian Walters of Manchester University asked me to do when I was employed by him, 'Rekindle the love of education in children'.

The school as an institution will need to be very clear about the behaviours that should be exhibited by the adults employed there in the promotion of its pedagogy. The behaviours required by those involved in educational delivery and the behaviours the learner needs in order to be successful will need to be understood, communicated and promoted at every opportunity, in an open, honest and pragmatic manner, devoid of blame.

As a qualified teacher with over 35 years' experience, I am increasingly questioning whether I was taught to teach a subject or pupils. I know my teacher training equipped me to do the former. The teaching of pupils came later. Learning that pupils need the right environment at school in order for them to learn came later still, through my own personal and professional development. This learning process continues to this day and for me it is the joy of belonging to the profession. The fact that we never fully master all the pedagogical protocols, and that there is always a new challenge and a colleague who has a better way of accomplishing what I am trying to achieve with pupils, keeps the profession vibrant. I will always require access to schools and teachers because this is where practitioners acquire behavioural expertise and Still, Every Blinking Day (SEBD!), I make mistakes!

For me, the process of learning to teach children or developing a successful pedagogy was school-based, ad hoc, and the result of patient managers who allowed me to make mistakes. Meeting two excellent trainers of teachers Bill Rogers and John Robertson, was a turning point in the development of my own teaching skills and pedagogy. I was also fortunate enough to be with teachers and managers who, in the main, liked and respected children and were willing to share their very evident skills with me. Not all teachers are so fortunate!

Our current education system appears to be very good at preparing teachers to deliver curriculum content. The system encourages the sharing of good practice in this area. However, in my experience in training thousands of practising teachers, I do not feel that we are as good at sharing good practice in terms of pedagogy. This apparent flaw in our system causes some teachers, through no fault of their own, to be ill-equipped to meet the learning demands of an increasing minority of challenging, disaffected and disengaged pupils in our school population.

I have learned from pupils and colleagues that the process of teaching is not about doing something *to* pupils. Teaching is doing something *with* pupils. Empathy for the learner assists in developing a fundamental partnership, where teachers provide opportunities for learning through an understanding of the pupils they are teaching. Understanding where pupils as learners are in society is another key in planning for disaffection and disengagement. I feel that this aspect is often missed out in developing the platform, the pedagogy upon which to build this understanding. That is the purpose of this book.

1 Beware Experts!

'A child's current behaviour often reflects an essentially sane response to an untenable set of life circumstances.'
(Madge Bray 1997)

Beware those who claim to be experts in the field of pupil behaviour! I do believe, however, that teachers can be experts in this field because they are doing the job every day. Many teachers have become excellent at sharing appropriate curriculum content. What teachers are sometimes not good at, usually because of time constraints, is sharing with colleagues their successful pedagogy. These are the behaviours and procedures teachers employ in developing classroom and whole-school environments; where pupils develop appropriate emotional and social interaction and become successful and satisfied learners.

I believe that pupils who are socially, emotionally and/ or behaviourally disruptive, disaffected or disengaged are also behavioural experts. Their field of expertise lies in knowing, either consciously or subconsciously, how to get teachers off-task and how to maximize peer-group 'kudos'. This process is employed to meet their needs, at the cost of high-quality teaching and learning time. At worst, schools employ enormous resources and energy in attempting to quash the efforts of this increasing minority of pupils. Fortunately, there are many excellent adult practitioners in schools. They are well aware of the behaviours employed by this group of pupils. They are also very adept at channelling these pupils' efforts and, almost by default, include them in the school's pedagogical process.

Such teachers are the experts in adult/pupil behaviour management. We shall explore the qualities and characteristics of these teachers in detail elsewhere. For now, we can say that they plan for different pupil behaviours as well as planning for curriculum delivery. They also attempt to plan for the outcomes resulting from pupil interaction, in advance of situations arising.

In extreme situations, I have known teachers who develop personal scripts and recording devices designed to keep lessons flowing and pupils on task. The pupil with social, emotional and behavioural difficulties (SEBD) is included in this planning process. For these teachers, SEBD pupils are not seen as a threat but as an opportunity to develop their own skills. These self-reflecting teachers understand that no matter what they do, some pupils will, Still Every Blinking Day, attempt to undermine what they do!

SEBD pupils, often without any personal malice or forethought, engage in the activities they do, simply because that is what they do! Their drive to behave this way is often found to be external to the school context. Behaviours exhibited by them are expected of them by their peers and, at worst, can be compounded by the pedagogy they receive.

It is very important to remember at this early stage in the book that most pupils are still wonderful! Many come from very supportive home backgrounds, regardless of any differentials. This being the case, developing systems that inhibit such pupils in order to constrain the unacceptable behaviour of the few who are disengaged might possibly lead to increased frustration and possible disaffection for pupils who are good students.

In the UK today, we have schools where many teachers learn to share appropriate adult behaviour in the development of their good learning relationships. Sometimes, this sharing can take place in the staffroom. If the staffroom exists, there appears to be two distinct types. There is the staffroom where, following an altercation with a child, a teacher can steam in and 'off-load' to colleagues. These colleagues will, in turn, based upon their own valuable experiences of pupils, listen, offer tea, biscuits, a seat and often advice on how they might approach the child in the future. This is a good staffroom, a place where teachers having behavioural difficulties with pupils are:

- listened to
- empathized with
- cared for (given a seat, tea and biscuits!)
- advised of helpful ideas and strategies that work with particular groups or individuals.

If we accept Madge Bray's assertion that children's behaviour reflects their 'life circumstances', we have the first building block in the development of our appropriate learning environment (1997). I believe that children are children are children. They have always 'been' and will continue 'to be' throughout time. It is our adult response, as teachers to children as learners, that might assist them in accessing the school system, regardless of their peripheral life experiences, genetic, racial and cultural differences.

Children live what they learn

If children live with criticism,
   They learn to condemn
If children live with hostility,
   They learn to fight
If children live with ridicule,
   They learn to be shy
If children live with shame,
   They learn to feel guilty
If children live with praise,
   They learn to appreciate
If children live with fairness,
   They learn justice
If children live with security
   They learn to have faith
If children live with approval
   They learn to like themselves
If children live with acceptance and friendship
   They learn to find love in the world

These words, taken from Roffey and O'Reirdan (2001), provide a reminder to us all of the influences we have upon pupils.

Roffey and O'Reirdan also remind us that:

Children don't bring only their lunch boxes and PE kit to school, they bring along a very large package of experiences, expectations, knowledge, skills and understanding.

In the 'good staffroom' and the 'good school', this is understood naturally. A good school is a collegiate place, where all teachers seek to include as many pupils as possible in an interesting and meaningful school experience. Here, staff bring their 'baggage' to school as well as the pupils. This is recognized. There is still a framework in place that allows the educational process to take place.

It would be naïve of me to suggest that this environment will succeed in supporting and successfully educating all pupils. I suggest that it will succeed with most of them. Such school environments exude corporate working practices and give clear messages to all pupils, staff, parents and governing bodies regarding acceptable and unacceptable working practices. Most new pupils and staff quickly and easily assimilate such a system. In the best schools, a conscious effort is made to induct pupils and staff into these working practices.

However, what if the staffroom is of a second type, a place of work distribution rather than collegiality? What if there are no opportunities to experience, listen to or even observe colleagues good classroom practices? In a similar scenario to the one above, where a member of staff steams in, expressing their displeasure regarding an individual or group, the response is often very different. Colleagues may stare at this individual and retort, 'Oh, we have no problem with him/her/them!!' This is a school environment where each adult goes his or her own way, behaviourally. Mixed messages of acceptable and unacceptable behaviour are given to often already confused pupils, parents and staff, particularly those who are newly appointed. Such confusion, from my observations, results in a lack of corporate direction and can erode the learning environment. This erosion is particularly noticeable in terms of time thus taken away from senior managers in school. They are expected to 'deal with' the disaffected and disengaged. In such school environments, basic behaviour principles are unclear and behavioural standards can sink to lowest common denominators. It is very similar to the concept purported in the parable of the bundle of sticks which is:

United we stand, divided we fall.

Working together in school, giving clear messages and responses to behaviour, is possible and achieveable. It is more problematic in wider society. However, it does appear that adherence to corporately agreed and understood behaviour in a school results in an improved learning environment.

Recently, I worked in a school with newly qualified teachers. I was aware that across the corridor from where I was working were several classrooms. As the day progressed, I observed the behaviour of a male teacher through the glass-partition wall. By the end of the day, I could guarantee that his teacher responses to his learners were resulting in an environment where he was very much in control and disruption was not taking place in the classroom. The reason for my certainty was that as pupils arrived at his door, a select group were loudly greeted with:

'Get out, you're not coming in here!'

I do not know where these pupils went, but there were several of them barred from entering his classroom each lesson. The remainder of the pupils were treated to a loud diatribe, all lesson, for five 'shows' a day. I know this to be true as I was there all day! When the pupils were 'released' from his lesson, they appeared like zombies with an almost post-traumatic stress syndrome demeanour. I felt sorry for this teacher as he was about my age – no other reason! I also felt sorry for him as the energy he employed in subjugating his pupils was going to take its toll on him physically, over time. Lastly, I felt sorry for his colleagues, especially if they had the class after him!

Was this a member of staff in the second staffroom scenario? It probably was, as he could say, with impunity, that he didn't have problems in his classes. Disruptive pupils never got in there! However, where did they go and who picked up on his poor management of them whilst they were out of his lesson? It worked for him, but was his teaching style fair on his colleagues in the creation of a learning environment? What would have happened if all the teachers had acted like this at that school?

I believe, nevertheless, that we cannot blame the teacher for acting in this manner. His school environment allowed him to continue behaving in this way. He had become entrenched in a set of behaviours that helped him to survive in the classroom every day. Without direction, support, advice and continuous developmental training, many teachers resort to this type of demanding behaviour.

The adult behaviour exhibited in this example stems from sheer force of personality. Or was it an example of an adult bullying pupils into submission? Was this teacher supported, observed or monitored and, in particular, advised upon his classroom management skills? Who assisted in advising him on his professional development and performance management? Was there a corporate, behavioural message being promoted in the school? Did pupils and parents understand and support the behavioural message and was the governing body aware of it?

In the past, when respect was integral to the role of the teacher and when society was very different, the behavioural norms and expectations of pupils and adults in school were also different. Today, there are very few of those behavioural norms in place. Schools have to state, explicitly, what is required of pupils, parents, teachers, auxiliary staff and governors. This is an important process that needs to be ongoing, in order to meet the changing behavioural demands made upon the institution of the school. If successful, the learning environment is easier to manage. Everybody is involved in agreeing the necessary behaviours. They are also involved in the development of the consequences that are accrued for compliance or non-compliance.

Developing an agreed, understood and accepted set of behavioural norms at school is a building block on the learning platform. Another is knowing where children are, in terms of their:

- Conduct Behaviour
- Emotional Behaviour
- Learning Behaviour.

This will be further examined in detail in Chapter 5.

Teachers need to consider the weave of the above behaviours with individuals and groups of pupils as it will assist them in their understanding of what they need to teach. It is a prerequisite in teaching and learning for these aspects of behaviour to be understood and valued. Teachers who ignore this fact will resort to the negative behaviours exhibited by the demanding teacher illustrated above. If allowed to continue, those who bully pupils into submission give a clear message that bullying is acceptable when done by adults. There will probably be a bullying issue in such schools.

Similarly, if we accept that most behaviour is learned, it would appear to follow that disrespectful teacher behaviour can result in disrespectful pupil behaviour. It could be argued that schools get the pupils they deserve!

Teachers need to build a teaching and learning platform upon which to deliver the curriculum to pupils. Schools and their teachers need to know the behaviours that they are required to promote in pupils. Initially, the school will need to agree these behaviours and the manner in which they promote them. Such recognition by a school body makes every adult in that environment an expert in behaviour.

If adults at school are given the opportunity to share their successful behavioural practices and, similarly, express what has not worked too well, in a supportive context, that school will capture good behaviour and appropriate pedagogical skills as aspects of the development of the learning platform. Such schools corporately become aware of adult behaviour that does not work. Such institutions don't waste valuable time alienating pupils because of their ineptitude. Such a school environment is an ideal one in which to capture and involve the pupil in further developing the learning platform.

Summary

- Sharing good practice develops appropriate teacher/ behavioural transactions.
- Observing positive role models as an aspect of professional development assists in improving teacher/ pupil transactions.
- Confrontational styles of teaching often get in the way of learning.
- Developing platforms of mutual respect creates improved opportunities for pupils to access teaching and learning.

Thus:

- Pedagogy is the key! (Rayner 1998)

2 Questions and Dilemmas

'Is it me or is it them?' (R. D. Laing 1970)

In reading Chapter 6 of *Emotional and Behavioural Difficulties* (Visser and Rayner 1999), I attempted to think through the questions and dilemmas that arise from classroom and school behaviour management principles and practices. In this chapter, 'Questions and Dilemmas', I consider the education of pupils who do not want to be in school and suggest that, for them, their school days are not the happiest days of their lives. Our dilemma, in an age of educational inclusion, is how to engage such pupils. Disaffection by pupils in schools, more recently termed 'disengagement' by central government, is possibly the greatest challenge for today's educationalists.

School context

Recently, I worked with a well-respected academy in Scotland. I asked staff to individually consider the question: What are the key behaviours in lessons which you consider to be the most irksome and disruptive? Their responses were well-considered. When ranked, they provided a basis upon which to consider current and collegiate school working practices. I will explain further the details of this process in Chapter 4 of this book. My reason for including them here is to highlight the heart-felt response of the head of English.

He is a long-standing, well-respected member of the teaching staff. Satiated in a love of his subject, he generously infects those pupils around him with a similar enthusiasm. I was privileged to be able to sit in and observe one of his lessons with a 'difficult' group of pupils. The lesson was a textbook example of what a teaching and learning environment should be. Pupils were fully involved and interacting appropriately with their peers and the teacher. The exercise was an analysis of the lesson's planning. On the surface, all pupils appeared to understand the purpose of the lesson and the subject matter that had to be absorbed. They were compliant, involved and respectful to the teacher and each other.

I later read his response to the exercise: 'What if . . .?' This is where all staff complete this question and in doing so, describe the one key behaviour that is most irksome and disruptive. They are then asked to consider what they currently do about it, both long and short term.

This teacher struck a cord deep within me. I believe that his response will also ring true with many other teachers. He said, in effect, that he did not have so-called behaviour problems in his lessons. For him, teaching was, in the main, a joy. However, his request was for help in motivating and including the pupils who complied by attending and minimally participating in his lessons. Such pupils, he added, were not without ability but, frustratingly, did not complete assignments and were unforthcoming in lessons. They were the pupils who 'glazed over' and disappeared into 'another world' and never achieved their true potential, due to influences beyond the classroom.

To this teacher's dilemma, I have no easy or fool-proof answer. I do know, however, that human beings are, in the main, social animals. I also know that norms of behaviour are important to groups. If these behaviours are reinforced, through expressions of their value by the group, they are more likely to be repeated. This is not to say that the classroom and school environment can address all of society's ills or motivate all pupils. Schools can however establish collegiate and valued norms of behaviour. The institution can communicate these behaviour principles and promote them to pupils and their parents. It is, therefore, important to be clear about which behaviours are to be valued and promoted throughout the school.

Clarity in communicating and promoting behaviour that assists teaching and learning is, I believe, a step towards involving more pupils in their education. Attempting openly and honestly to explain to both carers and pupils the behaviours that are required for pupils to be successful at school, and in the classroom, is a necessary aspect of this involvement. The dilemma for many teachers is which behaviours should the school and we, as teachers, promote? Many teachers also question their ability to promote these behaviours and ask whether they should be promoting them as an aspect of their job.

Training implications

The ultimate aim might be to teach all adults involved in ongoing, school-based behavioural transactions what their role in this process actually is. This training would initially identify the staff involved and ascertain their training requirements. Such whole-school training would hopefully attempt to establish common behavioural goals with the staff team and attempt to equip them with the skills to deliver agreed behavioural objectives. Equipping staff with skills and behavioural objectives in this way, should result in a confident, corporate team.

In my opinion, educational training establishments and institutions involved in the training of adults for work in schools should be required to consider the following questions:

- What are today's pupils like socially and emotionally?
- What 'mindset' do they bring to school?
- How do I as a teacher get them ready to learn?
- What are the behaviours required by the learner to access teaching and learning?
- What are the pupil behaviours that I need to manage?
- How do I balance the flow of the lesson against the behaviours of the pupils?

- What are the skills required by the practitioner to assist the learner in acquiring successful classroom behaviour?
- Where do I go for help with the above?

Pragmatic courses for adults working with children, based upon the above premises, would assist in creating more confident teachers and more time for curriculum content.

I attended a teacher-training college in the 1960s. I was in receipt of three years of training for a Certificate of Education. During those halcyon days I learnt a great deal about my subject areas and developed an interest in child psychology, amongst other things! The latter subject, 'Child Psychology', was included within a subject area entitled 'Education'. Minimal time was allocated to this significant area.

I was taught to break down subject material into bite-sized curriculum chunks. This was during the era of programmed learning and binary mathematics! At no time do I remember being taught how to teach children. Like my contemporaries, I was taught to deliver subject matter.

The resulting legacy, I feel, results in many of today's teachers asking the question 'What do I do if . . .?' in relation to pupils' behaviour in the classroom. The last 35 years have seen many changes to the profession and many new demands being made upon it. I suggest that one key question results from this:

'Am I a subject teacher or a teacher of children?'

Increasingly, as I work in schools, I find teachers still battling with this question. Their lament is still: 'I was not taught to teach children, I was taught to deliver a subject!'

Other questions that I get asked by practising teachers are considered below.

Is corporal punishment or confrontation ever acceptable?

Is it any wonder that some teachers base their current working practices on the role models of the teachers who taught them? Typically, some teacher behaviour is a hangover from a much more authoritarian period when 'might was right'. Children were to be seen and not heard, and respect for teachers came with the job. So often in my work in schools, I hear teachers explaining how, when they were children, if they went home from school and told their parents that they had got 'the cane' from a teacher, they would be further chastised by their parents. Some teachers feel that this is the root cause of school indiscipline, that is to say, lack of parental discipline and support for action at school. I would agree, in part, with this assumption but would suggest that society has changed. The behaviours that they experienced when they were pupils are now, in many instances, outlawed! I would ask teachers to consider why such physical and confrontational approaches have been deemed to be counter-productive, not just at school but in the wider community.

In a Class of Your Own

I remember attending a retirement celebration for an excellent headteacher. His retirement speech was succinct and to the point. He welcomed the gathering to his celebration and added, 'Ladies and Gentlemen, I can no longer use my cane, so I have decided it is time for me to go. Have a wonderful evening. Thank you for coming. Good night.' He went on to become a magistrate . . .

Sadly, the issue of corporal punishment is still uppermost in some teachers' minds. There still exists in the UK today a strong belief that bullying pupils into submission whilst at school is an acceptable means of controlling pupils. In the numerous conversations that I get drawn into, some adults' opinions appear to confirm this. I have come to realize that adult behaviour that seeks to control pupils through bullying and fear can work, but only in the short term. The effects of such teacher behaviour are very short-lived. They are ultimately counter-productive.

I have found confrontational pedagogy to be most counter-productive when attempting to develop the platforms of mutual respect. This respect is essential for teachers if they are to successfully deliver the current curriculum content to the majority of pupils. My ongoing concern is that teachers who discover that confrontation works well, albeit in the short term, will continually return to these strategies because:

- They know nothing else.
- It can be successful, in the short term.
- Such strategies require little or no planning.

- They believe that pupils should be well behaved anyway!

The danger is that such strategies and ideas can often result in equally confrontational behaviour being exhibited by pupils, the results of which are an escalation of both undesirable adult and pupil behaviour. More importantly, it does not provide a long-term solution.

Confrontation, if employed as a last resort, will need to be delivered in an assertive not an aggressive manner. It needs to be skilfully employed. The confrontational teacher who says to a class, 'Do that again and there will be trouble!' is enticing some pupils to consider:

- 'I wonder what he means by trouble?'
- 'This could be better than his lesson!'
- 'Shall we push him/her to find out what they mean by trouble?'

Similarly, when teachers are told to 'F*** off' in a lesson, they, rightly, address the pupil assertively and confrontationally, but perhaps without thinking through the outcome. If their response is: 'What did you say to me?' This could invite a repeat response. The situation can then escalate at the expense of teaching and learning.

What should be the response to unacceptable classroom behaviour?

Unacceptable behaviour must be addressed appropriately by the teacher in order to give very clear messages to pupils and their parents. Pupils and parents receive such confused messages about the acceptability or un-acceptability of some behaviour. This is often per-petuated by prominent members of our society. It is essential, therefore, to have thought through the out-comes before such behaviour occurs.

Have those outcomes been clearly communicated to staff, pupils and parents prior to them being employed? If not, the school as an institution needs to do so as a matter of urgency. Extreme, challenging and attention-seeking behaviour must have planned, known and agreed outcomes. Time spent establishing such para-meters gives the practitioner confidence in dealing with such behaviours. Their actions cannot be called to account because the outcome is already known, agreed and established.

This is the essence of behaviour planning. It results in established policy which is based upon consultation. It is vital, in my experience, that senior managers seek to establish behavioural parameters and support practi-tioners. If such parameters are challenged or crossed the agreed sanctions MUST be employed.

Finally, if any form of exclusion is employed as an out-come of such behaviour, it is important to have thought through a re-entry strategy. The aim must be to re-engage the pupil in the educational process as quickly as possible. It is also important that re-entry strategies are reasonable and acceptable to those in receipt of the initial behaviour. This will avoid further distress or resent-ment by that individual. Invoking a response to pupil behaviour is much better when it is established and planned for corporately, prior to incidents occurring.

Is it me?

I have observed some teachers providing a platform upon which some pupils perform, to the detriment of their lessons. Pupils sometimes develop these 'platforms' to improve peer-group kudos and avoid curriculum content. We have all heard of the 'class clown' and of parents who say that their child was only having a laugh.

In my own work, I have also found that violence breeds violence and aggression breeds aggression. It is no accident that our police force will, in the first instance, often send one officer into a violent affray. I am told that low-level responses often result in a de-escalation of potentially explosive situations. This produces a climate where rational intervention is more possible and likely to be successful. An individual officer can often diffuse an already over-heated situation, whereas a large force may incite further aggression, simply by what it represents.

Teachers need to develop skills that starve confrontational positions taken by pupils and at the same time maintain their dignity and integrity. This is more likely to be achieved by their asserting of authority, with confidence, in a professional manner within an agreed, known framework supported by the school. Teachers are less likely to resort to confrontational pedagogical styles if they feel that their responses to behaviour are supported by agreed policy. This should be a well-communicated and approved policy, developed in advance of the incident and employed as agreed.

What are the behaviours that disrupt teaching and learning?

Ofsted (2005) evidence states that:

- The great majority of pupils in school behave well, enjoy learning and work hard.
- The most common form of poor behaviour is low-level disruption of lessons, perpetuated much more often by boys than girls.

This would suggest, therefore, that most schools are not in crisis. Many teaching and learning situations are behaviourally well-ordered. Given the right set of circumstances, most pupils can learn, want to learn and exhibit only low-level disruption.

I would suggest however that, as Lord Elton (1989) discovered in his research for the *Discipline in Schools* report, published by the then Department for Education and Science, teachers are, in the main, not being beaten up in British schools and classrooms. Lord Elton pointed out that the majority of behaviour being managed in schools on a daily basis was low level but often high frequency. The different types of behaviour reported by secondary teachers that they had to deal with during their classroom teaching over a week were as follows:

Type of behaviour (listed by frequency of occurrence)	At least once a week (%)	At least daily (%)
Talking out of turn	97	53
Calculated idleness/Work avoidance	87	25
Hindering other pupils/Distractions	86	26
Not being punctual	82	17
Unnecessary, non-verbal noise	77	25
Persistent rule infringement	68	17
Getting out of seat without permission	62	14
Verbal abuse to other pupils	62	10
Rowdiness	61	10
Cheeky remarks or responses	58	10
Physical aggression towards other pupils	42	6
Verbal abuse to staff	15	1
Physical destructiveness	14	1
Physical aggression to staff	1.7	0

Lord Elton, in alluding to the increased pressures being placed upon teachers and schools by central government, referred to the number of new educational initiatives teachers and schools were expected to assimilate. This led to a plethora of books being produced, relating to the management of teacher stress. I consider one of the best to be *Managing Teacher Stress* by Bill Rogers (1996).

Lord Elton, like many researchers in this field, discovered that pupils were about the same as they had always been in terms of their behaviour and attendance. Ken Reid (2000) suggested that behaviour and attendance had remained the same despite numerous

31

government initiatives. What had changed and continues to be very evident in our schools is the ongoing pressure on schools to be adaptable, to assimilate changing trends and also the behaviours exhibited by pupils.

Historically, schools can be excellent at undertaking this and what is often lacking, in my experience, is the recognition of this. Increasingly, the inspection process (Ofsted 2005) appears to be supporting this by recognizing that in 2003/4 of 90 per cent of the schools inspected, behaviour was at least satisfactory. Worryingly, this had reduced to only 66 per cent in 2004/5.

To assist the teacher in responding to the above, it is important to remember that there are some constants or truths that the professional should consider:

- Teachers' behaviour influences pupils' behaviour.
- Teachers with effective classroom control are skilled at de-escalating problem behaviour and returning to the curriculum content.
- All teachers have the power to make classroom situations better or worse, behaviourally, through their interventions.
- All teachers can and should develop and learn control techniques as an aspect of their professional development.
- The 'self-reflecting' teacher is able to assimilate new skills into their working practices.
- 66 per cent of behaviourally disordered pupils 'spontaneously recover', no matter what you do (children grow up!). (Topping 1983)

What constitutes low-level disruption?

Returning to the advice given to me whilst at college, this is the key question I required answers to upon my entry into a school/teaching environment. I needed to know Still, Every Blinking Day, the key groups of behaviour that I should be aware of and plan for in advance of those behaviours being exhibited in my presence. Much deliberation could take place and many INSET days will have been taken up in this deliberation!

From my observations, the two key groups of behaviour that disrupt teaching and learning are:

- Attention-seeking behaviour
- Challenging behaviour

These are the two normal groups of human behaviour that teachers manage in schools and classrooms on a daily basis. In the main, these behaviours are managed well. Attention seeking is a normal expression to gain recognition from adults and peers. The response by those peers and adults to that behaviour is what modifies it into, hopefully, an acceptable social interaction.

Similarly, challenging behaviour should assist an individual in establishing themselves, autonomously, in a group without creating offence and respecting the rights of others to their autonomy. This is assertive or positive behavioural interaction. If misconstrued, misunderstood or misused, challenging behaviour can lead to bullying, intimidation and the oppression of the rights of others or their own autonomy. Pupils need to be given clear parameters of what is acceptable and unacceptable.

Lord Elton (1989) and Ofsted (2005) suggest that low-level disruptive behaviour could be categorized as pupils:

- talking out of turn
- avoiding work
- hindering the work of others
- being rowdy
- making inappropriate remarks.

These behaviours are often seen to be attention seeking in nature. The inexperienced teacher could respond to such behaviour by inappropriate interventions, giving rise to an increase in the very behaviour they were attempting to diminish.

Similarly, 'challenging behaviour' is a natural response to personal authority. Teachers who employ diversionary, de-escalating tactics in managing challenging behaviour will often remove the threat to the disruption. It is also important to make it clear to pupils that 'challenging' is not a successful behaviour to be used at school. It will be necessary for the teacher to follow up with a sanction during a period of calm rather than high tension. The sanction will give a clear message as to the unacceptability of such behaviour. Not to do so might give a message that such behaviour is acceptable!

What do I do about the above questions?

Teachers will need to become self-reflecting with regards to their pedagogical style. They will need to learn collegiate, supportive approaches from observing colleagues' responses in similar situations. They need to meet pupils where they are in terms of their:

- Conduct Behaviour
- Emotional Behaviour
- Learning Behaviour.

Summary

- Teachers need to identify the desired behavioural outcomes that they are working to develop in pupils.
- They need to be aware of the key behaviours that pupils employ in the disruption of lesson/teaching time and plan appropriately for them.
- They need to be aware of behavioural outcomes for pupils and promote an understanding of 'Compliance = Opportunity'.
- They need to have an ongoing, developing range of corporately understood and applied rewards and sanctions available to them.

Thus:

- Consistency of management is essential.

The questions posed have been included here because these are the types of questions that staff in schools seek answers to when they attend my courses. It is hoped that the following chapters will look in some depth at the concerns raised and, hopefully, provide some signposts.

3 What Type of Teacher Are You?

At times of crisis in the classroom, teachers have the power to make things better or worse.

(Bill Rogers 1995)

In Chapter 1 I described the teacher who dealt with problem behaviour by refusing to have troublesome pupils in his classroom at all and bullied the remainder into submission. Any pupils considered by him to be difficult, disinterested or disruptive were excluded from the lesson from the outset. Frequently, this pedagogical style causes more problems than it solves.

In my experience, fear works as an instrument of control in the short term. As a long-term strategy it is open to question and may lead, ultimately, to increased confrontation in the teacher/learner relationship. Rather than enhancing teacher/learner effectiveness, it leads to disrespect and a breakdown in communication. The 'mindset' of such teachers is that it is their job to *make* pupils learn rather than to *enable* them.

I feel that many teachers resort to this approach as they either choose to ignore other approaches or have never experienced or been taught the skills to embrace them. I feel reluctant to admit it but a very small percentage appears oblivious to the needs of both staff and pupils. If these same teachers have never had an opportunity to learn and experience alternatives during their training and careers, or have their working practices challenged, they continue to be confrontational. They may well have 'order', but what about effective and joyful learning? Is bullying by adults the correct behavioural message we wish to impart to our pupils?

Some pedagogical styles are more open to conflict than others. Rogers (1990) and Robertson (1990) explore these styles. And I would too like to reminisce here about my first day in the teaching profession, embellished now I am sure through, the rosy mist of time. Those halcyon days of the early 1970s, equipped with the confidence of a youth of the 1960s, I entered the profession in July 1970. Already there will be readers who will question this date but please have patience dear reader, as the significance of this date will become clearer as my story unfolds. I provide it as an illustration of how ill-prepared many of us were.

After three years at an English teacher-training college, the sum total of my knowledge in the area of the management of pupils' behaviour in the classroom had been supplied by a well-meaning tutor. When I asked him how I should address the pupil who was unwilling to learn or participate in lessons, was rude or ill-prepared for my subject, I was given the following strategy: 'Bill, go in hard, don't smile for at least six weeks and I'm sure you will be fine.' I am sure many readers received similar advice. You probably also, like myself, thought that such advice, although well meant, was ill-conceived and wholly inadequate.

I am sure most readers will agree that the two key groups of behaviour that disrupt teaching and learning are:

- Attention-seeking pupil behaviour
- Challenging (teacher authority) pupil behaviour.

This is not to preclude other behaviours that disrupt the teaching and learning process. However, my practice and observations have shown these to be the most frequently exhibited behaviours which can give rise to disruption. I shall consider the above in some detail in Chapter 4.

On my first day in the profession, I made an effort to comply with the understood stereotypical teacher mode of tonsure and attire. To readers in their fifties, you will understand me when I explain that I had folded and put away my Loon Pants, Kaftan and changed out of my Kalapuri Sandals. I was well scrubbed, smelt good and felt that I looked the part. I proceeded to my place of employment. Remember, I had only recently obtained a Certificate in Education, with Distinction! My success had led me to being asked to embark upon a new degree course: the Bachelor of Education (B.Ed.). I duly commenced studying for the entrance qualification. Unknown to me, an ex-president of the Students' Union had contacted his old college (mine) in desperation. He had had difficulty in filling a post at his school and in discussion with my personal tutor, my name

39

came up. The post was for an art teacher/housefather in the first purpose-built secure unit for school-aged, serious offenders in the country.

The ex-president of the Students' Union was now a deputy headteacher in this Home Office-managed establishment. It transpired that he had asked my personal tutor if they could recommend a student who could 'cope' with difficult behaviour. The previous incumbent of the post had failed to return from holiday and his whereabouts were unknown! To cut to the chase, six weeks later, following an intense interview process, I had the job.

My college tutor advised me against taking up the post as I would be specializing too early in my career. I know that my parents also had their doubts. However, when you are starting out and your are offered a starting salary well above the national average due to additional allowances, as a poor student you are at least tempted. The final inducement and deciding factor was that the position came with accommodation, cleaned daily, three meals a day, supper tray, washing and ironing, and linen changed twice a week. I jumped in with both feet.

On my first day, having undergone the transformation from 'hippy' to 'teacher', I received a phone call. I am sure in retrospect that the Home Office was very concerned about this newly qualified teacher taking a post of responsibility in their new, purpose-built establishment. It housed the most notorious, high-profile young offenders in the United Kingdom. Via this phone call, I was asked not to enter the establishment and that I would be met outside. I was met by a care worker who explained to me that he had secured his appointment because he had been a prison officer in Strangeways, now Manchester Prison. He explained how his skills had been transferable to this new position! He was of Scandinavian extraction and had an impressive stature. He was tall, strong and barrel-chested with a shock of auburn hair and matching beard and moustache. Given horns, he could have been a Viking! He explained to me that he had been assigned to 'look after' me. The reason given was that as he had an interest in water-colour painting and in the absence of an art teacher had been undertaking these duties. He also explained that he had had few problems! I later found out that his other passion was all-in wrestling, but I feel that is yet another story.

At this point, if you are a newly qualified teacher reading this, I don't know about you, but to be assigned a Viking to look after you for 'at least the first few weeks' was fine by me. To be further told by him that he would be going 'everywhere with you' (and he did, and he meant everywhere) was, for me very reassuring.

The Viking and I went into the establishment. If any readers have been to prison, for whatever reason, you will be aware that there is usually a double door to keep the residents inside and to protect the public. The Viking had the keys and we went in. This is the purpose of the tale: I was to be introduced to the two above-mentioned 'attention-seeking' and 'challenging' behaviours from a pupil within the first few minutes. I wish to illustrate how, after three years of training and the commencement of an advanced degree course, ill-prepared I was to address these behaviours. I feel many colleagues are in a similar position today and everyday!

I was unaware at this time that if a pupil was unruly in class in the secure establishment, they were sent to a 'quad' area just inside the double door entrance. Here, pupils were to stand in a prescribed manner. They were also supervised by a duty member of staff for this purpose. There was a cherubic male youth of about 14 standing as prescribed, with feet shoulder width apart and hands clasped behind his back. No mention was made of the youth by the Viking. I was left alone with this pupil whilst 'my protector' went to open the Art Suite and display the current work being undertaken.

As the Viking disappeared, the demeanour of the youth changed from strict compliance to inquisitiveness. Looking around him, the youth came over and, looking me in the eyes, told me to 'F*** off!' He was very pleased with himself and took up a stance often observed in Gainsborough paintings, arrogant and self congratulatory! You can imagine that, as a young chap of 21, I was far from impressed. I began to hear the sound-track from the *Psycho* movie shower scene in my head. I have to admit that the 'red mist' was beginning to cloud my judgement! My internal voice was shouting to me that I should admonish the youth for the indignity that I had just been subjected to. I felt like doing serious physical damage to this individual! Fortunately, I didn't. After all, I was by this time a consummate professional of about 5 minutes. I turned, dropped my arms from the aggressive stance that I was about to take and strutted, turkey-fashion, away from the situation, all the while shaking my lower arms and hands. The pupil, in this context the behavioural expert, was well used to finding the behavioural 'Achilles heel' in adults. He had trained for this moment over time in order to survive. For his efforts, the pupil had managed to get a newly qualified teacher to undertake a 'back-turn' and a 'turkey-walk'; minor stuff for an expert. The experienced teacher reading this will be well aware of what happened next!

In order to consolidate his position, the pupil, who for his efforts had managed to provoke only a minor adult reaction, proceeded to enter into the secondary phase of his onslaught. It was at this point that I was in receipt of the full attention-seeking/challenging mode from the pupil. As he had received little in the way of castigation for his previous efforts, he launched into a diatribe of foul language and gestures. I felt that I had no recourse but to carry out a response – any response! I had an advantage, as I had been shown around the establishment previously. I knew that in extreme circumstances an aggressive pupil could be escorted to another room and be placed there to cool down. I took this course of action. I 'escorted' the child to an empty room and closed the door. In effect, I isolated him.

The Viking returned to find me. Immediately he asked where the pupil was and what had happened to him. Some readers will have experienced senior colleagues questioning their actions in their dealings with the difficult behaviour of pupils. They, like me, will have sought to justify their actions, even though they thought that in the circumstances they were reasonable. I was no different. I blurted out what had transpired and how I had isolated the pupil. The Viking, obviously thinking of the child's well-being, said immediately, 'Oh, Bill!

Think of the paperwork! Our protocols require that we will have to inform the Home Office of your actions, the Social Services Department in the child's home town, his parents and/or carers and I [the Viking] will have to inform the Principal'.

I considered the advice from my college tutor at this point and also understood my parents' concerns, as I was almost literally marched from the establishment. I was thinking that my teaching career had been short but interesting! I was brought before the Principal. His prior training for his role as Principal was an extensive induction from the Home Office. He was quite literally the 'architect' in the development of the environment for the containing and rehabilitating of the very disturbed and disturbing youngsters housed in this new unit. He had been instrumental in introducing the therapeutic and psychological regimes and had considered every treatment programme. He sought the best available psychiatric and psychological advice which, in turn, was based upon the most up to date and current research of the day. The Home Office considered that his previous experience was also relevant in the establishment of this new post. He had been a war hero and was a highly decorated ex-Royal Marine Major! With some trepidation, I stood in his office with the Viking. Here, the Major, smelling sweetly of Old Spice, Grandee Cigars and peppermints, looked down upon me and with a twinkle in his eye and a wiggle of his prominent, waxed moustache said, 'Gribble, you will survive here! However, if you could learn a few skills whilst you are here, rather than instantly isolating pupils, I would be most grateful. You see, you may not have realized yet but these pupils have already been isolated from society!'

This was a sobering scenario. The key word here is 'skills'. I did not have the appropriate skills at this time to manage pupil behaviour. I do now, but like many colleagues, the behavioural experts with whom we work (pupils) often press my buttons and I, like you, can lose it and become just as distressed!

Preventative approach

Chisholm *et al.* (1986) suggest that developing a preventative approach to classroom disruption through the development of staff skills and pre-planning influences the amount of 'stress' or 'distress' they experience at school. The indicators and symptoms of stress offer an early-warning system to staff. In recognizing these symptoms staff can ideally develop individual and corporate strategies to combat distress.

Stress and distress

Students who break rules, disrupt others, refuse to do their work and are verbally or physically aggressive, make significant demands and threats upon school staff. The way staff react to those demands and threats at school is known as the 'stress' of the job. Everyone experiences stress at work and in their everyday lives. To some extent stress can be a healthy, even positive factor in our lives as it sharpens our wits and hones our skills. Positive stress is a state where stress is manageable.

This type of stress can be motivational and even enjoyable. Negative stress is that state where school staff, in this instance, feel unable to cope. This is distress.

The first step in coping with classroom disruption is to recognize, in oneself, stress and distress in the classroom or school. This quality, evident in the self-reflecting teacher, helps answer the question, 'What type of teacher are you?' With the ability to 'self-reflect' upon their state of mind a teacher is more likely to be able to address classroom disruption in a rational manner. Some staff will experience more stress in managing disruptive pupils than others. This is normal, but with collegiate support and training the extreme of 'distress' can be avoided.

Developing a 'positive' mental attitude or approach assumes that the way staff think about and interpret pupils' behaviour (staff attitudes) and the practical coping skills that staff have available to them will determine whether they will be stressed or distressed. These skills will include the following:

- A positive level of assertiveness
- A range of management techniques
- Self-awareness
- The ability to relax.

Signs of stress

- **Cardiovascular**
  Heart pounding, cold sweaty hands, high blood pressure, heart racing, erratic heartbeat, headaches (throbbing pain).

- **Respiratory**
  Rapid, erratic or shallow breathing, difficulty in breathing due to poor breath control, shortness of breath, asthma attack.
- **Gastrointestinal**
  Upset stomach, nausea, vomiting, sharp abdominal pains, constipation, and diarrhoea.
- **Muscular**
  Headaches, back/neck/shoulder pains, arthritis, muscular tremors, hand-shakes.
- **Skin**
  Acne, perspiration, dandruff, excessive dryness of skin and hair.
- **Malady**
  Allergy flare-up, susceptibility to infection such as colds, lowered immunity, skin rashes.

(Bernard 1987)

The philosophy underpinning a preventive approach is one which attempts to help school staff become aware of their own particular state of mind when entering into a behavioural transaction. This approach is simplified by the Preventative Approaches to Disruption (PAD) material developed by Chisholm *et al.* (1986), which states that:

- Pupils' behaviour is influenced by teachers' behaviour.
- Teachers with effective classroom control are skilled at avoiding and de-escalating problem behaviour.
- Specific techniques of classroom management and control can be described, practised and acquired by teachers.

- Teachers should take responsibility for developing their skills and should be supported in doing so by their schools.

A preventative approach, based upon the self-reflection of our personal interaction with pupils is, for me, a key aspect in the development of a platform of mutual respect upon which teaching and learning can take place. A most practical tool in assisting teachers in self-reflection is an ABC approach. This is considered in some detail in Chapter 4.

Some teaching styles are more open to conflict than others. Rogers (1990) and Roberstson (1990) explore these styles under the headings of:

- The Authoritarian or Demanding Teacher
- The Indecisive Teacher
- The Decisive Teacher.

I will add another style to this list:

- The Dignified Teacher.

The authoritarian teacher

In Chapter 1 I described this teacher. This is the teacher of subjects not children. Often, this teacher is an academic who came into the profession due to an interest in a subject area and not necessarily with respect for pupils' individuality. The teaching style of this teacher is an historical stereotype, and I do not mean 'Mr Chips'!

This teacher assumes a position of power over students. Power is used to control pupils and the vehicle employed is often sarcasm. A condescending manner is used to embarrass and ridicule pupils. This induces a state of fear in many of them. Fear works! However, the effects, as previously discussed, are counter-productive, short term and disengage many pupils who suffer such tongue-lashing. Fear is experienced by many of today's pupils and they have become adept at counteracting such attitudes in teachers and others.

In my experience, the employment of such a teaching style results in increasing levels of confrontation, poor working relationships and disaffection in pupils. The phrase comes to mind: '. . . and the worm turned!' Pupils do this also. After a while this confrontational style instils in some pupils an antagonism and attitude which is counter-productive to the teaching and learning environment.

A teacher employing this pedagogy might express the following:

- Students MUST obey their teachers!
- I am a teacher, they are only students!
- Pupils MUST do what I say!
- Children MUST obey their parents!
- I am an adult, they are only children!
- Students MUST listen when I speak!

The demanding and authoritarian teacher is open to high-level conflict from pupils who will not be 'quashed' in the above way. Teachers who interact with their pupils in this way are relying on what could be termed 'traditional authority'. Western society has taught today's children that 'respect' is earned. The 'traditional' teacher cannot expect that 'respect' will come with the position, as it may have done in the recent past. Teachers relying on traditional authority can cause serious confrontation in classrooms and wider confines of the school by attempting to gain a 'win–lose' position over some pupils.

> *A teacher who relies too heavily upon status to deal with challenges from pupils may face particular difficulties.*
> (Elton Report 1989)

As stated, in the short term many pupils will fear teachers employing this methodology to manage pupil behaviour. However, history demonstrates to us that when an oppressive rule of fear breaks down, anarchy takes over.

The indecisive teacher

This style is the antithesis of the demanding teacher. It can be equally damaging when attempting to maximize pupils' learning potential. The methodology attempts to give equal status to pupil and teacher. In so doing, the teacher assumes equal status, power and authority with the pupils who should be in his/her charge. This is not the 'Confident Classroom Leader' required in today's classrooms, as described by Peter Hook and Andy Vass (2002). This is the 'call me Dave' approach!

Pupils require parameters that are clearly devised, explained and adhered to in order for them to have the confidence to learn and attempt new things. This is the learning climate that the teacher should be attempting to achieve. If these parameters are uncertain it leads to a feeling of insecurity, or worse, pupils feeling unsafe. If this is the case the teaching and learning process *will* be impaired. The pedagogy described is what Wragg (1993) calls 'Permissive' and was epitomized by him in reference to A. S. Neill's educational experiments at 'Summerhill'.

A teacher employing this pedagogy may express the following:

- Teacher and pupils have equal status in school and classroom.
- To control pupils is repressive.
- We negotiate everything.
- All pupils are innately good.
- We don't need rules.

The decisive or positive teacher

This is the teacher who has thought through the concept of teaching or 'pedagogy'. This teacher understands that they are in control of certain elements in their school and classroom. They are involved in a process with their pupils but at the same time understand that they must lead and direct that process.

This acknowledgement of a need to lead is key. When I go on professional development courses, I often dislike the way some tutors organize their workshops. If there are discussion groups without leadership and direction they are, for me, opportunities for shared ignorance! As a learner, I want input, someone to look for and encourage positive aspects of my current knowledge and behaviour and lead me, at my rate of understanding, to an improved mental state and educational confidence. This is the pedagogical style that will minimize the opportunity for difficult behaviour by creating an environment where pupils:

- feel able to ask for clarification about tasks and activities
- are encouraged to find solutions to their own problems
- are listened to with interest
- receive consistent, positive feedback for effort, achievement and acceptable behaviour
- seek support from other pupils, as well as seeking the advice of the teacher
- receive explanations about what constitutes unacceptable behaviour but leaves self-esteem intact.

This positive approach will seek to prevent rather than treat unwanted behaviour and in doing so will aim to raise the overall quality of education for all pupils in the school, as discussed by Galloway and Goodwin (1987). The positive teacher will understand that at the root of difficult interactions is the behaviour of both parties. The elements under control are the teacher's behaviour but that behaviour will influence pupils' behaviour.

The decisive teacher understands that they can respond to unacceptable behaviour with anger but that this may escalate the situation. They also understand that they can respond in a calm, respectful manner, which it is hoped will help diffuse anger and assist in moving towards a resolution of a problem. Such teachers lead pupils towards desired behaviour which will assist them in achieving success in the classroom and in school.

In confrontational situations with pupils, this teacher has thought through the following before the situation arises:

- Where they are
- What they say
- How they say it
- Messages given by body language.

Key points that are evident in the behavioural transactions of positive, decisive teachers:

- *Voice:* Moderated, calm and firm
- *Audience:* Attempts to minimize the influence of the audience (peers). They will move away expecting compliance, they will attempt to remove the audience, gather facts and treat pupils as individuals.
- *Body language:* A calm, assertive manner which avoids intimidation, confrontation and respects personal space. An approach which is conscious of the effect of eye contact and facial expression.
- *Questions:* They use open questions. Short, sharp questioning can feel like an interrogation.

- *Listening:* Really listening, with calm interest, before interjecting so that facts are understood.
- *Respect:* This teacher will avoid put-downs, sarcasm, personal comments and direct criticism of the pupil, especially in front of peers.
- *Follow-up:* All unacceptable behaviour will be followed up. This may not be instantly but in the rational time of the teacher. The teacher will have developed pre-agreed, long-term and short-term interventions and consequences to behaviour with pupils prior to needing to employ them. Follow-up will be CAUSED by the pupil not IMPOSED by the teacher.

The characteristics of this pedagogical style are:

- The legitimate balance between the rights of the teacher as well as the pupil. Teachers have 'rights' too!
- The clear impression to pupils that the teacher is the 'authority' in 'authority'.
- The teacher will 'acknowledge' rather than reward appropriate behaviour.
- The teacher will seek to develop a platform of mutual respect upon which to build a teaching and learning environment.
- The teacher will be a self-reflecting planner for behaviour who will clearly communicate behavioural expectations and consequences but will be prepared to modify approaches as circumstances arise.
- They will be aware of their pupils' behaviour in terms of conduct, emotional development and learning style.

The dignified teacher

This is the teacher who remains calm and in control, rising above challenging situations by maintaining composure and professional principles.

Summary

- Teachers should aim to be the significant adults in the classroom.
- They have a legal duty of care over the pupils they have in their charge, which includes keeping them safe.
- Care should extend to giving positive direction in terms of education and behaviour.
- Teachers are society's vehicles. As such they should promote the standards and values of that society.
- The school, as an aspect of that society, should have clear behavioural aims that it openly promotes in supporting the positive, decisive teacher.
- In turn, this teacher is duty bound to support the school in the process of maintaining the school's behavioural ethos.

Thus:

- Teachers should aim to be decisive and positive in their transactions with pupils.

4 Skills

A winner takes the big problem and separates it into smaller parts so that it can be more easily manipulated; A loser takes a lot of little problems and rolls them together until they are unsolvable. (Harris 1973)

Developing classroom management skills becomes easier with experience. However, there is a danger that although some skills appear to work, they are effective only in the short term. Examples of short-term management skills are:

- fear
- intimidation
- bullying
- ridicule
- sarcasm
- put-down.

All will work with varying degrees of success in the short term. Over time, however, these 'skills' prove to be counter-productive. That is to say, they may have initially helped teachers to survive until break time but in the long term they give rise to antagonism and confrontation, thus feeding challenging behaviour in pupils. Developing appropriate skills that work over time is the ideal and more difficult path and there are no 'quick fixes'.

Teachers will always need to revert to some aggressive/assertive behaviour in their behavioural dealings with pupils. The greatest skill is in selecting and matching teacher behaviour to pupil behaviour. Failure to recognize that the use of the 'quick fix' though the employment of short-term, confrontational behavioural strategies will often lead to these very behaviours being exhibited by pupils at a later time. Someone previously downtrodden often seeks revenge. Lord Clifford warned King Henry VI against rough treatment or 'lenity and harmful pity', saying:

To whom do lions cast their gentle looks?
Not to the beast that would usurp their den.
The smallest worm will turn being trodden on,
And doves will peck in safeguard of their brood
Shakespeare: Part 3, Henry VI
Explanation in James Rogers (1985)

The worm will turn, and when it does the teacher might ask what role they played in this turning. Becoming a 'self-reflecting' teacher is a necessary prerequisite in the development of a teacher's pedagogical skills. A teacher who can continue to question their working practices is, in my opinion, the teacher who will actively seek to acquire new skills. Senior managers in schools must nurture this element of skill acquisition as an aspect of personal, professional development.

With regards to the development of appropriate behaviour management skills at school and in the classroom, Bill Rogers (1990 and 2002) suggests that the promotion of peer support for teachers can fulfil four functions in this process by:

- Enabling teachers to discuss common concerns affecting professional life.
- Providing opportunities for reflection on practice and problem-solving.
- Enabling the exchange of ideas on curriculum teaching methods and ways of dealing with pupil behaviour.
- Developing approaches to classroom management.

Primary and secondary behaviours

There is a body of evidence that suggests that behaviour in the classroom is influenced not only by the pupils' behaviour but also by classroom environment, and Rogers (1998) highlights this and further suggests that there are primary as well as secondary behaviours interacting in classroom and wider school and social settings.

Primary behaviour is the task in hand, for example, the teaching and learning in the lesson. The secondary behaviour is that behaviour which surrounds the 'journey' to the primary behaviour. This behaviour is the 'nuance' or low-level behaviour which either enhances or detracts from the process by which we reach the primary objective or behaviour. I term this process the 'transition' and devote Chapter 6 to a consideration of this. For the purpose of this section, it is enough to be aware that there are at least two levels of behaviour that interact with each other and if teachers get too involved with secondary behaviours, they do so at the expense of the primary behaviour.

For example, Topping (1983) found that in lessons where there were positive, secondary behaviours, in this case positive language, and if they were employed on at least a four positive to one negative ratio, on-task or primary behaviour was more likely to be adhered to. Promoting appropriate secondary behaviours which result in adherence to primary tasks or behaviour is a fundamental tool available to the teacher. However, it will only be available if the teacher is prepared to consider the following in developing their skills base.

Teaching appropriate behaviours

Teach behaviours that assist in enhancing teaching and learning, not interrupting it. Look for opportunities to teach desired behaviour by telling pupils what you want them to do rather than telling them not to do something. Rather than saying to a pupil: 'Don't run!' try: 'Walk please, thanks.' This approach requires a behaviour to be exhibited by the pupil.

Be assertive not aggressive

Calmly (a mental state required before entering into any behavioural transaction!) explain the behavioural expectation. Repeat the command if necessary (tactically ignoring the secondary behaviour in order to concentrate on the primary behaviour as mentioned above and explained at length in Chapter 6). Pupils will model adult behaviour. They are programmed, psychologically, to do so. If the teacher is calm and in control pupils will eventually model that behaviour. Keep comments short and avoid long explanations and arguments.

Throughout history we have seen how violence breeds violence and aggression breeds aggression. The aggressing teacher will set an example to pupils that will, over time, be counter-productive.

Catch them being good!

Topping (1983) found that positive comments relating to pupil behaviour created a more positive, on-task learning environment. Teachers should actively look for and acknowledge appropriate pupil behaviour, without patronizing or embarrassing pupils. It is suggested that at least three times as much attention should be paid to acts of appropriate behaviour. Teachers should aim to 'catch pupils being good and tell them, when acknowledging their behaviour, that this is what is expected "in our classroom"'. This gives behaviour cues to other pupils and will assist in channelling 'attention-seeking' behaviour (see p. 66).

Plan

Below, I suggest that teachers planning for behaviour can be assisted by employing an ABC model, the psychology of which is explained below. If teachers are aware that a pupil or group of pupils behave in a particular manner, they can work out their responses and consequences in advance. Having done so, it is a good idea for the teacher to discuss this with the group. They can explain that if certain behaviours are exhibited they will accrue either positive or negative sanctions. Further, teachers can point out to pupils that if they employ inappropriate behaviour in class it will cause them, the pupil, to cause something to happen. It is the pupils' choice! Discussing individual and group consequences with pupils will ultimately give teachers more time to teach.

Follow-up

If a teacher develops a plan and discusses it with pupils, the teacher will need to consistently apply the agreed outcomes. To err in the process of applying the plan will negate the planning process and break trust with pupils. The inevitability that a teacher will follow-up both good and unacceptable behaviour with appropriate acknowledgements, rewards, sanctions and consequences will 'make or break' the plan.

The ABC approach

The basic psychological concept of Antecedent, Behaviour and Consequence (ABC) is a useful tool available to the teacher. This 'self-reflection' process helps in planning for behaviour and in reflecting upon behaviour in previous lessons. Such behaviour, of both pupil and teacher, needs to be understood in terms of its primary and secondary interaction, as outlined above. In pedagogical terms, apart from curriculum content and planning, this 'ABC' concept can be described as follows:

A – Antecedent
What you did as a teacher and confident classroom manager to find out and reflect upon pupils' behaviour before your lesson, with consideration of the possible causes of this behaviour.

B – Behaviour
What behaviours were exhibited by pupils and teacher following the consideration of A? What did the pupils gain from or display through their behaviour?

C – Consequence
What did you do to follow up on these behaviours? How do you plan to improve on aspects of 'A'? What are teachers' responses to pupils' 'behaviour in context'?

This planning model will be considered further in Chapter 5 as an aspect of developing teacher self-control.

I have found this approach incredibly helpful in my own working practices. On my better days, I am able to question myself and, without anxiety say, 'Is it me?' This thought process takes pressure off the teacher and increases the hope that things can get better. It gives both a vent and a direction to difficult classroom situations. Things can get better through such planning, which can give rise to:

- Improved skills acquisition
- Avoidance of pupil traps
- Ownership of one's own behaviour
- Appropriate addressing of pupil misdemeanours
- Improved lesson planning through the inclusion of behavioural planning
- Development of long-term and short-term consequences
- Increased confidence
- Improved self-esteem
- A lowering of stress levels.

It is suggested that if a concerted, collegiate, corporate ABC approach is employed in school, pupil achievement would improve.

Control and transaction

As the learner needs to prepare/be prepared for learning, so too does the teacher need to prepare for teaching. To do this the teacher needs to think of teaching as the sum of two parts: control and transaction. If they do this, they can consciously employ the development of a rapport or relationship with pupils, as a pre-requisite or building block of the learning platform.

An understanding of how these two aspects of successful teaching interrelate in developing rapport or relationship is liberating. It enables the teacher to own their own behaviour and not that of their pupils! This understanding will also provide the teacher with the other vital ingredient they will require on a daily basis: confidence in their working practices. The confidence to say, 'I am alright. What I am doing is fair and has worked well on previous occasions.' Such confidence will be further enhanced if classroom management procedures have been discussed and sanctioned by colleagues and pupils, and incorporated into school systems and communicated to parents.

The equation thus reads:

Control + Transaction = Teacher Confidence

For me, these two areas in the development of pedagogical skills are hugely important they will be explored and developed further in Chapters 5 and 6.

Developing the fourth 'R'

The skill of developing curriculum knowledge is vital for all teachers. However, curriculum knowledge alone is not enough in today's classroom. There has to be a major change in the mindset of the many teachers who came into the profession to teach and promote the subject that they both know and love. To those who blame schools for the current state of child behaviour in society many teachers would respond by saying it is a parent's job to discipline children and a teacher's job to educate them in their subject area.

However, with no extra training and little consideration for the profession, today's teachers are expected to teach pupils, not subjects. This important distinction is evident in the good working relationships that develop between teacher and pupil, but, I would suggest, many teachers would reject that this is their responsibility.

The teacher who invests in Wragg's (1993) Fourth 'R' – the 'Relationship' – is today's 'Aware Teacher'. The teacher who understands the demands made upon the profession by Western society will attempt to develop, with colleagues, pupils and parents, a platform of mutual respect upon which teaching and learning can take place.

Teachers continually make the point that they are required to get through a prescribed National Curriculum and that they do not have time to spend in the development of the type of skills that I am advocating. Teachers often swim a National Curriculum tide and may not achieve any lasting, long-term, behavioural change that assists pupils in their learning process. What I suggest in this chapter is that the teacher who invests in the development of a 'platform of mutual respect' as the basis of their pedagogical style will create more time to deliver the curriculum and more time to understand individual pupils and how they learn. Belief in this, I believe, is the basis upon which today's teacher needs to build their skills in the classroom.

By way of example I provide the following personal scenario. For many years, if a pupil threw their work on the floor, adding an expletive, I would loudly demand that they pick it up again. I thought that this battle of wills was more important than the flow of the lesson. I did not realize that my confrontational demands:

- Were more disruptive than the misdemeanour
- Took time away from the compliant pupils

- Took up valuable curriculum delivery time
- Could have been exchanged for a non-confontational response
- Eroded my personal dignity at the expense of my pupil/teacher relationship.

Now, by actively seeking to develop my pedagogical skills base, I am better prepared to achieve an on-task outcome, be a less-disruptive teacher and retain my personal dignity.

The two key behaviours

When teachers plan for their lessons, it is increasingly clear to me that lesson objectives will not be reached if a plan for behaviour is not developed too. Topping (1983) suggests that a consideration of behaviour appears to be a sensible place to start when planning a lesson. If we, as teachers, accept this, the next thing to consider is the behaviours we need to plan for. I suggest that there are two key groups of behaviour that, if left unplanned, will disrupt lesson flow. I have deliberated extensively with colleagues to reach this conclusion and we continually return to:

- Attention-seeking behaviour
- Challenging behaviour

Attention-seeking behaviour

I have worked with teachers who say:

'How do I stop them talking through me? It is as though
I don't exist!'

To address this, the teacher will need to understand that
they can make a difference. Peter Hook and Andy Vass
(2002) seek to help teachers become more confident.
In their excellent publication *Confident Classroom Leadership* they suggest that at the beginning of the journey
towards confidence, teachers need to:

- *Take responsibility:* both personally and professionally
  for your working environment and the development
  of your skills. Move away from a blame culture and
  look to yourself to make things better in your classroom for you and your pupils.
- *Take action:* it is up to you to effect change. Develop
  your own skills and be prepared to take risks and
  make mistakes.

  The most helpful realization that I came to early in
  my career, largely because I had followed a drama
  course while at college, was that it was alright for
  me to make a fool of myself in front of pupils. They
  rarely noticed anyway and, if they did, acknowledging my behaviour and at times apologizing for
  my actions assisted in the development of mutual
  respect.
- *Keep an open mind:* teachers are on a journey – for
  some teachers the journey is never-ending as there
  are always new challenges and ways of doing things.

Hook and Vass appear to be suggesting that the power
of the group can be channelled by the good leader.

In a Class of Your Own

This is a teacher who is assertive, has a clear vision and exudes confidence but is prepared to admit their faults and mistakes. They continually consider the balance between behaviour and lesson flow, have agreed consequences and rules, and understand where they are and where they are going in behavioural transaction. Such teachers minimize the opportunities for attention-seeking behaviour to become an issue by ensuring that they do not give pupils platforms upon which to display their behaviours. They are wary of the 'W' questions in public forums.

The 'W' questions are:

- Where (have you been?)
- Why (are you doing that?)
- What (do you think I feel about that?).

If I present the attention-seeking pupil with an opportunity to respond to me in front of peers following one of the above questions, for example, 'Where have you been?' I may very well get a pupil response which ridicules me as the teacher and promotes the pupil in the eyes of their peers, such as: 'Why? Have you missed me?' Similarly, when asking: 'Why are you doing that?' a pupil may respond with: 'Because it gets on your nerves!' Finally, to ask a pupil: 'What do you think I feel about that?' could invite, from some pupils: 'Do you think I'm bothered?'

Attention-seeking behaviour needs to be managed and if possible minimized for the sake of lesson flow. John Robertson (1990) recognizes this and coins the term 'tactically ignoring behaviour' (TIBING). This is a useful skill in managing pupil behaviour. It does not totally ignore the attention seeking or disruptive behaviour employed by pupils or groups of pupils but it does give the clear message that:

> 'For the sake of the lesson, I, "the teacher" will not become involved, but at some point in the near future I *will* follow up and you, "the pupil", will understand that you have caused some sanction to be imposed.'

Robertson also introduced me to the concept of 'least intrusive teacher behaviour to most intrusive teacher behaviour'. The concept is discussed in detail in Chapter 6, 'Transaction', but to explain briefly here this is the establishing of a series of steps by which the teacher can monitor their behavioural transactions with pupils and have a range of skills and sanctions available to them through an accumulative planning approach. This approach helps to prevent teachers from making inappropriate responses to pupil behaviour. It is a way of developing a rational hierarchy of responses. This concept fits well into the ABC planning model, described above.

A similar hierarchy of intervention is promoted by Smith and Laslett (1993) for what they term 'on the surface' behaviours. This is similar to Bill Rogers' understanding of 'secondary' behaviours (2002) and is useful in helping teachers to manage the group of daily exhibited, low-level behaviours that I term 'low-level attrition'. If we are not careful, these behaviours grind us down. If teachers ignore these behaviours, they can lead to higher forms of disruption. Planning to use a range of low-level, planned teacher skills in advance of low-level disruptive pupil behaviour being exhibited will often employ reverse psychology. This is teacher behaviour that gives a message to pupils that:

- I am not being drawn into your behaviour but I will address it in my way, in my own time.
- I will not be shocked but I will be proactive in closing down your behaviour in a pragmatic manner that keeps the lesson flowing.
- I will be fair, assertive and will employ respectful working practices (even though you may be disrespectful).
- I will ensure that if you attempt to spoil my lesson I will keep following up and, with colleagues if necessary, impose sanctions that you, as a pupil, have caused to happen.
- I will tell you that you are wonderful, but what you are doing is unacceptable and you, the pupil/s, have put me in a position where there is no alternative to doing what we agree that I have to do.

This 'Arnold Schwarzenegger' approach of being unable to do something now but 'I'll be back' provides the clear prompts and parameters that so many pupils require and imposes known consequences to unacceptable (and acceptable) behaviour.

If all staff agree on their responses and apply them in a consistent manner, then the behavioural message or code of conduct in the school or classroom will be understood quicker and complied with sooner.

Challenging behaviour

Olsen and Cooper (2001) suggest that interventions that would assist the disruptive teacher in developing a less-challenging and more positive learning environment should involve the adopting of the 'Four M' approach as developed by Smith and Laslett (1993). This is not to say that seriously challenging behaviour requires instant, corporately agreed and supported responses. I have, however, found that the agreement to implement set strategies (and why not those that have been tried and tested) is certainly a lot easier than developing individual strategies for behaviour.

The 'Four Ms'

Smith and Laslett suggest from their research that it would appear that the management of challenging classroom behaviour is more successful when combining the skills, knowledge and understanding of the wider context of the school. The 'Four Ms' are envisaged as an interlocking and overlapping set of headings that provide quick 'aide memoirs' for the teacher, especially at times of crisis.
  They are:

- Management
- Mediation
- Modification
- Monitoring.

Simply put, the teacher will need to manage situations through the developing skills. The main skill will be the ability to mediate, but at the same time retaining the ability to manage and close down situations so that a lesson can continue. Through reflection upon the situation, the teacher can modify pupil behaviour through rewards and sanctions. Teachers may also need to consider and modify their own behaviour. Finally, through a process of self-reflection, they will be able to monitor the success or otherwise of the approaches employed and adapt them accordingly. This procedure will, it is hoped, provide fewer opportunities for challenging behaviour to develop by giving very clear behavioural messages and expectations.

The three teacher types proposed by Smith and Laslett (1993) are similar to those described in Chapter 3. They are:

1. Imperturbable
   Vigilant teachers who do not expect pupils to misbehave. They have a positive attitude and have developed clear boundaries and consequences.
2. Resilient
   Non-vigilant teachers who are more flexible in their approach but have clear boundaries and follow up misbehaviour.
3. Disruptive
   Teachers with adversarial, confrontational approaches that produce negative attitudes in pupils, where discipline is confused with order, conformity and obedience, thus negating efforts to instil a baseline of behavioural expectations.

In relation to the 'Four Ms':

- *Management*
  There are four rules:

  i.   Rule One   'Get them in'
       Establishes a clear understanding of who you are
       as a teacher and where the pupils physically
       should be within the classroom.
  ii. Rule Two   'Get them out'
       Establishes a routine for the end of a lesson.
  iii. Rule Three   'Get on with it'
       An appropriate learning material, content and
       teacher manner – the 'transaction' (subject of
       Chapter 6).
  iv. Rule Four   'Get on with them'
       The teacher knows their pupils and is aware of the
       'atmosphere' through being 'mobile' in the class-
       room (another aspect of 'transaction').

  It is not difficult to relate these rules to the different
  teacher types and to see how each will either enhance
  the opportunity for good classroom management or
  encourage confrontational, challenging behaviours.

- *Mediation*
  This is again dependent upon teacher type. The
  'resilient' teacher is perhaps the best suited to developing approaches that will mediate with the more
  persistently disruptive pupil. This will be attempted
  in order to minimize persistent, disruptive, pupil
  behaviour. To achieve a balance between the flow
  or pace of the lesson and intervention is a real skill.

As referred to above, Robertson (1990) calls this skill 'tactically ignoring'.

- *Modification*
  This requires the 'self-reflecting teacher', possibly employing the ABC approach, to modify or change their teaching style or the learning environment to meet the needs of their pupils. Smith and Laslett (1993) envisage this as being a 'behaviourist' approach and would include considerations of:

  - Description (of behaviours being exhibited)
  - Observation (who, where, when, how often, how serious)
  - Reward (acknowledgement, praise)
  - Punishment (logical consequence, pre-agreed sanction).

  The 'disruptive' teacher would be unlikely to be able to undertake this procedure.

- *Monitoring*
  Monitoring the outcome of interventions, especially teachers' feelings in relation to their levels of:

  - Anger
  - Anxiety
  - Conflict
  - Depression.

There is an obvious need for behaviour-management techniques to be employed in order to reduce these feelings in both pupils and teachers. If they are not, it may be that some teachers are unable to internalize

and exercise appropriate strategies and will, therefore, require collegiate help to achieve this.

Meeting pupils where they are at –
behaviourally

Meeting pupils where they are at, in terms of three
aspects of behaviour, as outlined by the Qualifications
and Curriculum Authority (QCA) in 2001, would appear
to underpin this aspect of teachers' skills development.

In 1999 the QCA commissioned researchers from
the University of Birmingham School of Education to
undertake a project to develop criteria that schools
might use for measuring pupils' emotional and behavioural development. Following an extensive review of
the range of criteria used for assessing emotional and
behavioural development by educational psychologists
in Local Educational Authorities (LEAs) in England, the
researchers developed a set of criteria to support school-
improvement strategies. This process was enhanced by
a consultation exercise and resulted in a set of comprehensive criteria to address three aspects of behaviour:

- Conduct behaviour
- Learning behaviour
- Emotional behaviour

A period of research and extensive consultation resulted
in agreement upon five 'aspects' of positive behaviour
which acted as descriptors to each of the above. In
terms of developing skills, as a teacher, one needs to

know these areas of behaviour that must be developed in pupils if they are to be successful at school.

This identification of 15 key aspects of behaviour provides both teachers and schools with a clear set of behaviours that must be promoted by the institution if pupils are to access the National Curriculum successfully. Skilled teachers will promote these behaviours by considering where pupils 'are at' in terms of where they are in relation to the descriptors, and will move pupils, with empathy, towards these behaviours.

Cumbria County Council Education Service have taken this a stage further and have developed a 'Behaviour Curriculum' for Key Stages 1 and 2 (Michel 1998) and a 'Positive Behaviour Curriculum' for Key Stages 3 and 4 (Michel 2002). As tools for developing teaching skills, I find these innovation helpful and record this here in the hope that other professionals will also do so. If you are developing behavioural profiles or plans for pupils, these tools will enable teachers to develop their skills in helping pupils understand what they need to do behaviourally.

For teachers starting out, to be able to develop a base-line understanding of 'where pupils are at' behaviourally should assist immensely in their curriculum planning.

Developing consequences

The most challenging aspect in the development of all school- and classroom-based behaviour management systems is that surrounding rewards and sanctions. The first thing that springs to my mind is:

'Why should I reward pupils for doing what they should be doing anyway?'

I can empathize with the view expressed on *Question Time* some years ago by the retired Chief Officer of Her Majesty's Inspector for Schools, Chris Woodhead, when he said:

'Pupils have been "starred" out!'

Mr Woodhead explained that by his statement he meant that many pupils 'expected' to be 'rewarded' when behaving appropriately. He felt that this was counter-productive and gave the wrong impression to pupils. I have suggested, earlier, that as the significant adult and confident classroom leader, it is an aspect of the teacher's role to point out, or to acknowledge, appropriate pupil behaviour. To do this is to provide cues for other pupils. These are expectations and not rewards.

Similarly, a teacher needs to be able to say to pupils:

'You are lovely but what you are doing is foul/unacceptable and by your actions you will *cause something to happen!'*

The consistent application of the 'this will happen' aspect of the negotiation, by all staff, is often the stumbling block of behaviour-management systems. The skill is the consistency.

77

Rewards and sanctions – planning for the 'what ifs?'

I have found one successful whole-school way of developing rewards, sanctions and the pedagogical protocols necessary to underpin the successful behaviour-management system. I call this process 'Planning for the what ifs?'

1. All adults in a school context who come into contact with pupils are requested to write anonymously on the top of a piece of paper: 'What if?'
2. With this focus they are then asked to consider, in relation to the pupils with whom they interact, the 'What if?' that for them as individuals gets in the way of their work. Examples could be given such as:

   'What if they are late?'
   'What if they continually talk?'

3. Following a short period of personal reflection and without consultation, all adults are asked to write down their one most irksome 'What if?' on their piece of paper.
4. When completed, the adults are requested to turn over the paper and write the following questions, leaving a good space in between to fill in their answers:

   'What do I do in the short term with regards to this behaviour?'

'What do I do in the long term if this behaviour continues?'

5. Ask all adults to, individually and without consultation, write in their answers to their two questions. Allow time for reflection.
6. When completed, progress can be made in several ways. As a consultant, I would collect the papers and conduct an analysis which could result in something similar to the chart below. This is an actual example from a small secondary school.
7. The first aspect in the analysis is to look for similarities and group the responses accordingly. In this case the similarities fell into:

   - Low-level 'attention-seeking' behaviour
   - Low-level 'challenging' behaviour
   - Being equipped for the lesson
   - Timetable changes and interruptions

At this point it might be helpful if we relate these finds to research. Ken Howell (1998), in looking at variables influencing pupil behaviour, suggested that teachers concentrate upon those that they can influence, at the same time being aware of the other variables over which they can have little or no effect. See Figure 7.1 on p. 155.

8. Making deductions based upon an analysis of the staff returns provides the basis for a corporate response. In this school 26 out of the 37 members of staff took part in the exercise who were concerned about low-level attention-seeking disruption

Behaviour that disrupts 'teaching and learning' and strategies employed from 37 staff returns

Rank	No	Behaviour	Short Term	Long Term
1	26	*Inattention/Attention Seeking* Talking, laziness, inappropriate comments or smells, not listening to instructions, ongoing, minor interruptions.	Wait for silence, Gentle encouragement, Attempt to prevent, Interval detention, Stop lesson, Address with pupil, Catch them being 'good', Remind them of the purpose of the lesson, Rule reminder, Refocus pupil, Give second warning, Monitor through observation (eyeballing!), Raise voice	Punishment exercise, Isolation in class, Detention, lunch-time detention, Employ school sanctions, Speak to individual, Use level 1 so parents are aware, Get depressed, Get frustrated, Try not to let the behaviour of a few effect the compliant children

2	6	*Confrontation/Challenging* Refusal to work, deliberately failing to follow instructions, answering back, having the last word.	Attempt to extricate pupil from group but in class, Attempt to address with individual in class but not at other pupils' expense, Attempt to tactically ignore behaviour	Move pupil/s to a side seat, Follow up in my way in my time, Refer to line manager, School discipline policy, Follow department and school policy
3	3	*Lacking Equipment* (e.g. pen, book, calculator, jotter, homework)	Reinforce the importance of bringing the correct equipment, Interval detention, Cause for concern	Lunch-time detention, School referral system
4 =	1	*Unruly corridor behaviour*	Verbal reprimand	SMT School referral system
4 =	1	*Timetable disruption*	Plan ahead	Tedious punishments, Lunch-time detention the following day

to lessons. This is a high proportion of staff and amounted to more than 70 per cent of the adult staff involved in the daily running of the school.

9. If I was a senior manager in this school, with this data, I would be concerned about this response. In acting upon the data I would seek to employ Bill Rogers' (1990, 2002) four principles, mentioned at the beginning of this chapter (p. 58). Based on the staff returns, I would make further opportunities available to enable teachers to discuss common concerns affecting their professional life. Then, I would seek to provide time during these sessions to reflect upon current practice and problem-solving. I would use the information provided by staff in their 'short-term' and 'long-term' responses as the basis and focus for discussion. I would be seeking a pragmatic hierarchy of interventions, to be agreed upon by all staff.

I would hope that agreement could be reached as to the appropriate nature of staff responses, the hierarchical structure and how staff would ensure consistent application of the agreed responses by all staff.

Enabling the exchange of ideas on ways of dealing with pupil behaviour will enhance curriculum teaching methods and allow more time to teach. It will be important to justify the time spent on this exercise in this way.

10. Developing approaches to classroom management cannot be a one-off exercise. This fact has been discovered by schools attempting to incorporate the excellent 'behaviour and attendance' materials

provided by the *Key Stage 3 National Strategy* 'Behaviour and Attendance Training Materials (DfES 2004b). The key message from the *Key Stage 3 National Strategy* to schools is the need to develop skills and incorporate current effective good practice in the area of behaviour management. There is also the aim to spread these practices amongst all staff in order to combat unacceptable behaviour and poor attendance:

- Improvements in behaviour and attendance require comprehensive whole-school actions. 'One-off' training sessions are unlikely to lead to embedded change.
- The behaviour and attendance strategy builds upon the existing range of school self-evaluation and improvement activities (QCA/DfES 2001).
- *All* adults within the school community should become skilled and active in improving behaviour and attendance.
- Behaviour and attendance improvement starts with staff understanding the causal factors and leads on to an appreciation of pupil needs.
- Improvements in behaviour and attendance will lead to an improvement not only in standards and inclusion but also in the quality of the day-to-day experiences for pupils and staff within schools.

Given this guidance, the staff returns can be employed as evidence of current need (i.e. in this case the starting point – low-level attention seeking disruption), current corporate and consistent practice (solution focused from staff returns short-term and long term responses).

Summary

- There is a clear link between the successful classroom manager who is able to keep pupils motivated and focused on the 'primary behaviour' and improvements in school standards of behaviour, attendance and academic success.
- This is a sensitive area but skill acquisition amongst staff should be an open and honest pursuit.
- The most serious incidents of misbehaviour are obviously those that cause the greatest distress and attract the most attention.
- Schools will need to be sensitive to the corporate,
- Collegiate support they provide and the strategies employed in dealing with situations that are often outside the staff's remit.
- In the acquisition of skills, it is important to remember the proverb:

  'Look after the little things to prevent them becoming big things'

- Attention to detail in the management of staff and pupil behaviour is vital.

Thus:

- Focusing on the development of skills to combat relatively low levels of misbehaviour will prove to be effective over time in lifting staff morale and pupil behavioural responses if consistently applied.

5 Control

Clients send messages through their non-verbal behaviour. Helpers need to 'learn how to read' these messages without distorting or over-interpreting them. (Egan 1998)

'Control' is, for some, a strong, even offensive and confrontational word to use in the teaching context. However, in this context, the concept of 'control' is to be considered in terms of:

'Who's in control of whom?'

As I have previously stated, I do not want teachers to be in control of children. However, I do want teachers to be in control of themselves. By doing this, teachers will create a controlled environment where pupils can learn to be in control of their own behaviour. They will then realize the benefits that this brings. Teachers should promote this simple concept in their classrooms:

'Compliance equals opportunity'

Bill Rogers (1995) has a mnemonic for controlling behaviour, YOYOB:

'You Own Your Own Behaviour'

He encourages teachers to ensure this in behavioural transactions. For me, an example of the teacher who is not in this state of mind and out of control would be the teacher who, following a difficult situation, says:

'If you do that again there will be trouble.'

This is a teacher who feels their back is to the wall. The behavioural experts (pupils) will recognize this and in some situations, I am sure, will 'sense' the teacher's fear. At the very least, these pupils will recognize the tension or atmosphere and use it to their own advantage. Some pupils, given such an outburst from a teacher, will consider the statement and after a short while will say to their peers:

'I wonder what 'trouble' is – shall we see . . .?'

It is likely that they will then push the boundaries because of the challenge provided by the teacher. This will be evidenced by increased disruption through the employment, by pupils, of 'attention-seeking' and 'challenging' classroom behaviour; much of which is directed at their peers.

Similarly, the teacher who is directly sworn at in a lesson can, quite rightly some would say, further disrupt the lesson by questioning that pupil's actions. This teacher response can give a 'platform' upon which the pupil can act out behaviours which are sometimes even more objectionable than the initial misdemeanour. The cycle played out might be: attempting to ridicule the teacher, gaining peer group kudos and avoid the curriculum content. The latter aspect, avoiding curriculum content, is a classic ploy used by pupils when the work is beyond them. Disruption is used to cover pupils' weaknesses in the company of their peers.

To exemplify this, a teacher came to me recently complaining that they had been sworn at by a pupil. When they asked the pupil to repeat what they had said . . . Do I need to say more!

The teacher who is in control of their own behaviour knows where they are going in their behavioural transactions. They balance incidents against lesson flow and have at their disposal long-term and short-term interventions which will ultimately address the exhibited behaviour. These interventions will:

- Not feed the behaviour or cause it to be repeated.
- Give a clear message to all pupils about acceptable and unacceptable behaviours.
- Intervene with appropriate consequences that are known in advance of them being employed.
- Leave pupils knowing that it is them causing something to happen to them, not the teacher imposing sanctions upon them.
- Leave pupils knowing that they are 'wonderful' but that their 'behaviour' is unacceptable.
- Teach that compliant behaviour results in increased opportunity.

This is what I mean by control. Knowing, in a controlled manner, how we will allow ourselves to react. This could be in situations where we are confronted by behaviour which is both disruptive on a personal level, and distracts from our teaching on a professional level.

In order to do this, as teachers we will need to be aware of the behaviours that pupils exhibit which could lead to such disruption and distraction. If we are aware in advance of these pupil behaviours, we should be able to plan, in advance, our reactions to them. This should limit the disruption and distraction they cause and quickly get the lesson back on track.

Teachers who survive until the next lesson after a difficult session might be heard to say:

'Off you go, and don't let that happen again!'

They will not break the cycle or address inappropriate behaviour. They may even encourage future difficult and disruptive behaviour. This is because there will be pupils leaving such lessons saying to each other:

'That was a laugh, what shall we do next time?'

Control and observation

Bower (1969), in his research into adolescents' mental health, strongly suspected that teachers who focused upon a pupil's observable behaviour in school and in the classroom were closest to an 'operational reality' than other professionals who conducted sedentary examinations. This is a little like the good referee who observes what is happening on the field of play and makes decisions accordingly. Where the poor referee will stick to the rule book and intervene at every observed infringement of the rule, the good referee will choose to ignore certain infringements for the sake of the 'flow' of the game. This is what I understand by an 'operational reality'.

Observation will assist the teacher in planning for behaviour. Wolfendale (1992) suggests that as an aspect of developing personal control, such observation can help the teacher to develop a dispassionate view of pupil behaviour. This, in turn, will help the teacher realize that pupils are not necessarily 'good' or 'bad' but are in fact exhibiting behaviours that have been learned externally to the school context and in some cases will be innate. It is the responsibility of confident classroom leaders to assist pupils in recognizing which behaviours will help them in the school and classroom context and which behaviours will impede their learning.

The competent teacher will also be aware that it is important to keep control of the 'lesson flow' and at times let certain observed behaviours go without intervention. These behaviours will, however, need to be followed up at some point.

I have mentioned developing platforms of mutual respect upon which teachers build their teaching and learning environments. Observation is a vital prerequisite in the development of this climate in the classroom. In maintaining a level of self-control, teachers who are aware of the influences over their pupils' behaviour will be much more rational in their own behavioural interaction.

I note here that in social-work training, student social workers value their training in behaviour observation as being the most important aspect of their course (Trowell and Bower 1995). Such training involves a consideration of children from the following perspectives:

- Child development
- Cognitive development
- Social interaction
- Psychodynamic
- Attachment
- Societal
- Current research
- National policy
- Culture, class, age, race and gender.

I do not expect teachers to become social workers. Schools are already in danger of becoming the most expensive department of social services, at the expense of the education process. However, there is an argument to suggest that a closer working relationship between local and national governments' children services could enhance the understanding for teachers of some of the extremes of behaviour, presenting in today's schools and classrooms.

I suggest that similar training elements could assist in this mutual understanding. This could lead to greater teacher tolerance and self-control. If these training elements are not present, the teacher should have the opportunity to seek assistance from their social-work colleagues. Ken Reid (2000) found that the best initiatives in attempting to change pupils' attitudes and behaviours, were those that were 'joined up' and had ongoing funding with different children's services departments, particularly at local level. If teachers and schools are to be influential in developing controlled environments where teaching and learning can safely take place, Children's Services must work in partnership with schools in overcoming the behavioural problems of the increasing minority.

As mentioned in Chapter 3, as a student about to go on my first teaching practice, like so many other trainee teachers, I asked:

> 'What if the pupils refuse to do my work, swear, and fight etc . . .?'

My personal tutor, who had not taught for many years, advised me to:

> 'Go in hard, don't smile for six weeks and you will be OK.'

During my three-year course, this was the sum total of my teacher training in behaviour management. Unfortunately, I meet teachers today who have recently been given similar advice by colleagues, mentors and tutors. Such advice is, of course, sadly inadequate and wrong. There is an increasing number of excellent graduate teacher training and university courses being taught. However, a common training and apprenticeship approach, alongside high-calibre mentoring support is not always available to all teachers entering the profession today.

Self-reflection

In maintaining a level of self-control, the self-reflecting teacher will need to develop a method of behavioural self-assessment. This will enable them to develop their skills, gain confidence and remain in control. The ABC approach, the psychology of which is explained at the beginning of Chapter 4, is a method I have successfully employed to monitor my behaviour and to develop self-control through increasing confidence in my transactions:

A – Antecedent
What did I do before a lesson to prepare for pupils' behaviour and direct my teaching and learning accordingly?

B – Behaviour
What behaviours (pupil and adult) were evident in my classroom/school compared to my planning? How did those behaviours enhance or impede the development of my learning platform?

C – Consequence
What did I do to follow up on that behaviour? Do I need a long-term plan? What consequences (rewards and sanctions) did I employ? How successful were the consequences I employed in assisting my teaching and focusing the learner?

Antecedent

When I was a new teacher, I felt it was my job to make pupils obey me and do as they were told. I was the demanding teacher. Through observing other teachers, I found that there was another way. I began to understand that it was not an 'us' and 'them' situation. I was part of a group, with a specific role. That role was to be the confident classroom leader. As an aspect of planning for behaviour, I need to include this attitude or mindset in my planning. To do so helps prevent me from being the demanding bully who attempts to dominate pupils. The teacher with an attitude of consciously attempting to dominate a group will erode teaching and learning time through the resulting confrontations, especially with adolescents.

As the confident classroom leader, I will know where I am going behaviourally, in advance of meeting the class. To help me in this process there are various strategies that I will employ:

Well-prepared lesson content

I will attempt to be well prepared academically. By this I mean that I will know what I am going to teach and the learning objectives that I am attempting to reach. I will obtain and have ready the equipment I require and will know how to use it. I will consider the methods I will employ to assist in making the material interesting and accessible.

Teachers, especially those new to the profession, are well-versed in this pretty basic process of lesson planning. However, there are some other basic tips that are sometimes missed.

Lesson location

I will know where the lesson is taking place and if I can get there from my previous lesson before the pupils. Being there first is a real advantage in establishing behavioural parameters. If you cannot get there, and you have a difficult class, see if it is possible to change the venue, if not this term then perhaps next.

Pupils' names

Know the pupils' names. Being anonymous in a group is an ideal opportunity for the disturbed and disturbing to cross the Rubicon from normal to abnormal behaviour. Overcoming the problem of anonymity for the teacher should be of paramount importance as an aspect of planning for behaviour as an antecedent. Planning in this manner can be achieved in numerous and sometimes cunning ways, but should ultimately lead to the teacher being able to put a name to a face and vice versa.

Pupil images

One way of achieving the goal of learning pupil names is to enquire if your school has a registration system that records not just names but a photographic image of the pupils. If it does, ensure that you have a printout of any new classes that you encounter, including the photographs. Pupils are amazed when you say their name following a request, especially if this is the first time of meeting.

Seating plan

Another way would be to have a printout of a plan of your classroom. With this plan, make sure that there is a space for a name above each seat. As pupils enter your class, ask one to write in all the class's names. Obviously, you want to ensure these are the real ones! The reward for this task is that the 'scribe's preferred seat is saved for them. Next, check that this pupil has done a good job and that there are no nicknames, derogatory names or purposefully misleading titles! I think you will find that 'Elvis' has left the building!

A pre-prepared seating plan with names already attached to seats is also a good idea. However, this method can lead to confrontation, which will in turn take up teaching time. The teacher will need to explain the 'ground rules' to pupils prior to entry into the classroom to ensure the success of this method.

Rules and routines

From the above, it would appear obvious that there is a need for the teacher to establish themselves as an authority, in authority, from the outset. To do this they will need to develop rules and routines that enhance teaching and learning opportunities and assist lesson flow and pace. Above all, they will need to develop rules and routines that pupils understand, respect and employ.

As teachers, we will need to know what these rules are. We also need to have planned our responses to rule infringement and pupils' classroom behaviour, so that our authority and dignity remain intact. The trick is knowing these rules, routines, consequences and responses in advance of entering the classroom.

For example, for my sins, I inherited an excellent name for a teacher: 'Mr Gribble'. I can now predict that with some classes, upon my first encounter with them, when I say,

'Good morning class, my name is Mr Gribble.'

a small proportion of them will pass comment and even fall about laughing! The way I approach this will affect all my future dealings with that class. If I respond hurt and angry, some pupils will enjoy the spectacle and will attempt to produce a similar response from me every time I meet them. If I have planned my response, I can maintain both my authority and dignity. I will learn (following a comment about my name or laughter) to respond with phrases such as:

'Very good, I haven't heard that one – I'll see you later!'

'I am glad to see we all have a sense of humour – I hope everybody is alright now!'

Such phrases should not invite comment but should show pupils that I am rational, in control and that I not going to be drawn into their games. I will return to this in Chapter 6.

For the moment, I will recommend that the development of a few pertinent rules with pupils at the beginning of an encounter is an important exercise.

To further develop agreed consequences with pupils for compliance or non-compliance is also an important stage.

Additional needs

It goes without saying that pupils with additional needs require more specific or specialized support in line with their individual and/or statutory requirements.

Teacher attitude

The teacher that understands 'where pupils are coming from' emotionally, socially and educationally will benefit from this during the teaching and learning process. This attitude will assist them in developing their platform of mutual respect. Further, such knowledge will increase confidence in the teacher and will help overcome feelings of intimidation. In Chapter 1, I introduced the phrase 'knowing where children are at' to explain how we develop platforms upon which teaching and learning can take place. Like all concepts, this was taught to me.

I was giving a talk on managing pupil behaviour in London. During the lunch break, a young African man came to speak to me and commented upon my use of 'meeting pupils where they were at'. He suggested that this was, for him, the most important aspect in the educational planning process. I thanked him for his observation and he went on to explain his reasoning. He said that he was working in London's East End with groups of adolescent African-Caribbean boys. Most had been excluded from school for substance abuse and violent behaviour. I verbally applauded him for his endeavours with this challenging work. He thanked me and went on to explain that he had been placed in the care of a Dr Banardo's home during his adolescence. He went on to say: 'If a teacher had not met me where I was at, I would have been on the other side of the desk!' I thought deeply about this. What did it mean to meet a pupil 'where they are at' as an aspect of my planning?

I have been helped in these deliberations, in relation to the aetiology, or causal links between emotional problems and learning difficulty, by the publication *Supporting School Improvement* (QCA/DfES 2001). Meeting pupils 'where they are at' is, for me as a teacher, to understand them in terms of their observable:

- Conduct behaviour
- Emotional behaviour
- Learning behaviour.

This work is based upon the ideas of Bloom (1976) who developed a model for school learning based on three similar influences upon pupil performance. As an aspect of planning, especially for groups of difficult pupils, teachers will need to understand this process in terms of the influences upon pupil performance. This is a vital aspect of the 'antecedent' in answering the question,

'What did I do before the lesson to make it go well?'

Conduct behaviour

Does the pupil understand the behaviours that they are required to employ in the context of the school, and are they similar to the behaviours they use outside school? Increasingly, it appears that for many pupils the behavioural expectations inside school are very different from those expected of them outside school. If today's teachers and managers do not give credibility to this fact, as an aspect of developing an appropriate teaching and learning environment, then by design or default they will 'exclude' pupils.

These pupils will not understand, know or will be allowed to ignore the required behaviours that are necessary to access formal learning.

In my lectures, I refer to the track by Status Quo: 'Whatever you want' (1980). For me its lyrics explain the mindset or attitude that many of pupils and adults actually have. I believe it is a mindset developed in Western, democratic societies. As an adolescent, I went through a time of earning and learning my human rights. However, we now appear to live in a climate where most people feel that they have a personal right to a certain level of material right.

I suggest that this is the mindset that influences many of our pupils' conduct when they come to school. It is a set of behaviours which are based upon instant gratification. Teachers, in general, cannot change society's behaviour. I do believe, however, that we can say to society and our pupils:

'When you come here, to this educational establishment, behaviourally, we do this.'

I feel that this statement is particularly necessary today. Anyone involved with learning theory will understand that today's society constantly promotes 'instant gratification' and the behaviours or conduct surrounding it. One such behaviour has been singled out by the advertiser when marketing goods for children, which is: 'Pester Power!' Children and advertisers know that the more they demand, the more likely they are to receive the 'instant gratification' they desire. We know, however, that learning is about '*deferred* gratification'. Educational establishments need to say:

'Some of the behaviours employed outside schools will not work here.'

'To enjoy your experience here, you will need to acquire appropriate behaviours.'

'You are not bad or wrong, but when we are here we do this.'

A strong, clear behavioural message must be delivered in a corporate manner by today's educational institutions. Such a message will need to give details about what behaviours are required. The QCA guidance (2001) provides such details in describing five aspects of 'conduct' behaviour that pupils will need to exhibit if they are to be successful in the school environment. These are:

- Behave respectfully towards staff
- Show respect to other pupils
- Only interrupt and seek attention appropriately
- Be physically peaceable
- Respect property.

In some cases, following in-depth observation and consultation, schools must be prepared to say to some pupils and their parents that they are not ready to access a classroom because they are not exhibiting the appropriate behaviours.

The school must, however, also actively seek to provide the opportunity for pupils and, if necessary, carers, to learn the behaviours that will lead to success at school. Attempts should be made to do this without affecting the self-esteem of either pupil or parent/carer.

An educational institution will need to consider the ultimate behaviour they are aiming to achieve, as an aspect of pupil conduct. Many schools have done this, but if you are in a school that has not, consider this for a moment. If you brought a child of your own to your current place of work, what behaviour, above all others, would you encourage, and, ultimately, what behaviour would you want them to exhibit in their daily lives? I suggest that you thought of 'respect' or an aspect of it.

Respect appears three times in the five aspects of 'conduct behaviour'. Let us consider the idea of 'respect' for a moment. At the centre of this concept is 'respect for oneself'. Without 'self-respect', how can groups and individuals proceed to the second level or layer – that of 'respect for others'? If this level is not internalized, then the outer layer is almost impossible to achieve. For me, this is simply:

  'Respect for the world and all that is in it.'

Some readers will be thinking of the arrogant youths who are disrupting their lessons, and will say that they have plenty of 'self-respect' and are very much in control of their conduct at school. To exemplify this, as a newly appointed deputy head teacher at a large residential school for pupils exhibiting social, emotional and behavioural difficulties (SEBD) I felt that my role (conduct) was to champion the behavioural causes of my colleagues in the school. When pupils were admonished for their behaviour, I felt my role was to support the teachers' actions. I did this by loudly and verbally castigating a pupil further, in the hope that my colleagues would hear me and thus feel supported by their senior management. On one occasion, the more I shouted at a particular pupil, the 'cooler' this individual became and, in turn, the more I shouted! I got to the stage where I felt a 'rip' above my heart, which hurt! I took a deep breath and stood back as the pain was so intense. This was a set of actions I should perhaps have used much earlier in my 'transaction'. The pupil, seeing my pain, placed his arm around my shoulder and said 'Are you OK now Sir?' So who was in control of that scenario and whose self-esteem and respect remained intact after that incident?

Such situations are, for the self-reflecting teacher, opportunities to consider new strategies. For this pupil the verbally aggressive teacher was pretty 'low down' on the threat scale – I needed another approach.

I needed to understand his conduct in relation to mine and meet him 'where he was at' and show him a successful path forward which would lead to his acceptance and understanding in the school's culture. This requires excellent communication and observation skills enabling the teacher to seek out which behaviours need to be encouraged. The strategies and their relevance should be explained to pupils. All this will need to be considered in advance of entering into lessons and classrooms as an aspect of the 'antecedent'. The teacher who is successful in this will, over time, develop the fourth 'R', the platform of mutual respect, upon which to build their teaching and learning in partnership with their pupils.

Emotional behaviour

I suggest that a pupil who is emotionally fragile is not generally 'available' for learning and development until they have the inner experience of 'emotional containment'. Paul Greenhalgh (1994) suggests that effective learning is dependent upon emotional growth, and Maslow (1954) suggests that there is a hierarchy of emotional states which he terms a 'hierarchy of needs' – see Figure 5.1.

For the teacher in school it is important to recognize the importance of 'emotional state' and 'emotional development' in their planning. QCA guidance (2001) encourages schools to develop the following five aspects of emotional behaviour in pupils:

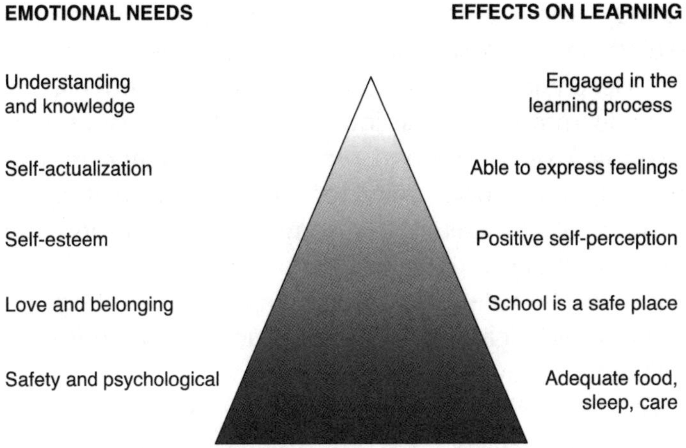

EMOTIONAL NEEDS   **EFFECTS ON LEARNING**

Understanding   Engaged in the
and knowledge   learning process

Self-actualization   Able to express feelings

Self-esteem   Positive self-perception

Love and belonging   School is a safe place

Safety and psychological   Adequate food,
                                                 sleep, care

Figure 5.1 A hierarchy of needs (Maslow 1954).

- Empathy
- Social awareness
- Happiness
- Confidence
- Emotional stability and good self-control.

Where pupils are coming from environments where these behaviours are not in evidence, or, at worst, ridiculed, teachers must take on a 'sanctuary mentality' as an aspect of planning in the 'antecedent' phase. Pupil should be able to come to school thinking 'Thank goodness I'm here', and not, 'I hate this place.'

Pupils who are relaxed in their environment and understand the behavioural parameters – what Ted Cole *et al.* (1998) term 'the rubber boundary' of the school – are pupils who are more likely to be receptive to a teaching and learning environment. Bob Spalding

(2000) went so far, with colleagues, as to develop 'quiet places' in schools through the Cheiron Project on Merseyside. One feature of the provision was to provide immediate crisis intervention for pupils presenting a lack of control and pre-criminal tendencies. This presented an opportunity for the development of an 'emotional curriculum' for some pupils in order that they might develop the appropriate behaviour necessary for them to access classrooms without disrupting the teaching and learning of others. Such interventions are necessary today more than ever.

Topping (1983) suggested that the 'on-site unit with a transition facility' was a cost-effective necessity for those schools which had pupils who required emotional support in order to access the wider school curriculum.

The pupil who comes to school emotionally scared, abused in their surroundings and not knowing why will be angry. They will not be receptive to a teaching and learning environment. As the QCA (2001) pointed out:

> *'Other aspects of pupils' development are of equal priority to their academic attainment.'*

In some cases the priority for pupils will be their emotional and behavioural development. Teachers must also admit that on a bad day 'emotional stability' and 'good self-control' are often beyond *them*, let alone their pupils. Having an educational environment that encourages the development of the emotional and behavioural skills necessary to access all aspects of school life will assist pupils in Maslow's concept of 'self-actualization' (1954). It will also promote a greater involvement in their acquisition of personal 'understanding and knowledge'.

The importance of developing emotional intelligence as the vehicle by which we deliver our innate gifts to society is well understood (Golman 1996). For pupils in a sterile, emotionless world, the valuing of personal 'understanding and knowledge' is an essential aspect in helping them to becoming human. How many of our schools' staff and government officials understand the importance of this aspect of the school's role in the development of 'rounded' human beings entering society?

Learning behaviour

I feel that this final area of behaviour, considered by QCA (2001), of the importance in understanding 'style' differences in learning behaviour, is perhaps one area where a great deal of recent progress has been made.

Most teachers, in planning for behaviour, will understand the necessity to allow for and accommodate for different learning styles in their lessons. However, I find that recent research in the areas of cognition and its causal link to learning, are further immensely helpful in the behaviour-planning process. 'Personal learning style' describes the way in which an individual habitually approaches or responds to the learning task. According to Riding and Rayner (1998) 'personal learning style' is comprised of two fundamental aspects:

1. *Cognitive style*: the way in which a person thinks.
2. *Learning strategy*: processes employed by the learner in response to the learning activity.

They postulate that a person's cognitive style is probably an in-built and automatic way of responding to information and situations. Furthermore, this is probably present at birth or most likely to be fixed early on in life, being certainly all-pervasive and affecting a wide range of individual functioning. A person's cognitive style is then, a relatively fixed aspect of learning performance and influences a person's general attainment or achievement in learning situations.

As teachers, we need to be aware of cognitive style and its aetiology to learning strategy when promoting for ourselves and our students an understanding of the five key aspects of learning behaviour (QCA 2001). These are:

- Good attention span and homework ethic
- Good learning organization
- Effective communication
- Efficient working in a group situation
- Appropriately seeking help.

Further, there are two style families of cognition: the 'Wholist-analytic' and the 'Verbal-imagery' dimensions. It is worth taking time to explore these ideas – see Riding and Raynor (1998).

It is possible to develop a 'pedagogical style' which encourages and reinforces the learning strategies of the pupils in the classroom, one where teacher–pupil interaction produces improved attainment and achievement. We can say with impunity that:

'Pedagogy is the key.' (Rayner 1998)

Dr Rayner suggests that this consideration has implications for the educational provision of all pupils. Teachers, in their planning of the 'antecedent' stage, will need to consider the:

- psychology of the learner as a learner
- role of the teacher's teaching persona
- individuality
- new forms of pedagogy
- support systems.

For school improvement, schools will require support in developing provision for all pupils in the areas of:

- individual difference
- human relations
- learning process
- curriculum differentiation
- pastoral care
- resource management.

Teacher behaviour

With behaviour-management skills, the teacher will also need to balance the skills for delivering lesson content. I call this 'the transaction' – the pragmatic manner in which teachers, whilst maintaining their dignity, can get their ideas across to others. The 'others' are pupils, who already have their own ideas and agendas. This will form the basis of Chapter 6.

Consequences

This final aspect of the ABC model considers how to follow up, self-reflect and introduce elements into antecedents (A) that will improve classroom behaviours both teacher and pupil (B). Developing consequences is a multidimensional task. There follows a consideration of what we need to do in the short and long term, as well as individually and collegially.

Short term

A range of teacher behaviours must be employed to keep pupils on-task and the lesson flowing. Current strategies of reward and sanction will need constant review in response to the behaviour exhibited by the pupils.

Long term

It is important to have full knowledge of behavioural parameters from the school behaviour policy and policy at local and national level. We will need to have a set of acknowledgements, rewards and sanctions at our disposal. It is useful to note observations of good and bad behaviour and possible responses which can later be referred to in the development of 'appropriate consequences'. This should assist us in 'engaging brain before opening mouth'.

Individually

We should actively develop rules that promote good lesson interaction and routine, and be prepared to monitor and change these rules when necessary. We should be prepared to keep pupils back after lessons, develop sanctions and rewards that are appropriate, and monitor behaviour in these transactions. When:

Giving praise
We will:

i.   be private, speak quietly and avoid embarrassment;
ii.   look directly at the pupil but we will not 'eye-ball' or stare;
iii. give a reasons for our actions;
iv.   make our responses feel personal;
v.   be genuine;
vi.   make life as enjoyable as possible.

Showing disapproval
We will:

i.   look at the pupil but remain calm;
ii.   speak calmly and quietly;
iii. give reasons;
iv.   label the act and not the pupil, i.e. 'you are wonderful but what you have done is dreadful';
v.   keep self-esteem intact;
vi.   listen to both sides of the argument;

111

vii.   be private, seeking to exclude other pupils from the interaction;
viii. find out how to keep a 'chronology' and make an appropriate Child Protection Referral;
ix.   find out how to have a case conference.

Collegially

We must know when to ask for help and not leave inappropriate behaviour unaddressed because we have run out of ideas or feel intimidated.

We must gather observed, behavioural facts upon which to develop our strategies with colleagues. Myths, legends, personal agendas and woolly perceptions hinder the development of strategic intervention and lead to antagonism and bitterness. We must call case conferences, invite in parents and other agencies and, with our colleagues, develop strategies that will assist all pupils in accessing the teaching and learning environment. We must remember that we do have the power to make things better.

We will need to understand that we will never reach the end of our journey in the development of behaviour management strategies. There is always another way or a new perspective. Our richest resources are our professional colleagues in school. We also have friends, our professional association and access to libraries and the Internet.

Summary

We are not alone on this difficult journey!

6 Transaction

'People don't care how much you know but they do know how much you care.' (Course delegate 2005)

Cooper and Upton (1990) found that the 'ecosystem' of the school or institution influenced behaviour. They suggested that the following could encourage unacceptable behaviour in both pupils and staff if evident in school:

- low teacher morale
- high teacher turnover
- unclear behavioural standards and expectations
- a lack of understanding of what constituted acceptable and unacceptable teacher and pupil behaviour
- inconsistent methods employed by teachers in addressing pupil behaviour
- poor whole-school organization
- a lack of awareness of individual pupils (especially the well-behaved ones).

Influences on transaction

Schools that are aware of their influence on behaviour are schools that can develop appropriate opportunities for learning. In this chapter, I am proposing that certain methodologies, attitudes and procedures in school will enhance or impede 'transactions'. By transactions I mean the processes by which a person with a body of knowledge (the teacher) gets that body of knowledge across to someone else (the pupil). I suggest that behaviour can be taught, learned and replaced over time in school settings.

This can be achieved by teachers who have clear 'preferred practices' which are promoted by the whole school, and who employ 'appropriate' behaviours in their 'transactions' with pupils and colleagues. The development or change in pupil behaviour is the result of interactions between the skills, experiences and prior knowledge that the pupil has brought to school, the demands made upon them and the support they receive in making sense of the school's behavioural expectations.

The Department for Education circular on pupils with problems at school, *'Pupil Behaviour and Discipline'* (1994), suggested that successful whole-school policies for the management of pupil behaviour should exhibit the following characteristics:

- They should be simple, based upon a clear and defensible set of principles or values.
- Mutual respect is a useful starting point in policy development. (Sadly, this phrase was used only in

114

the guidance document, DfE 1993, and was removed from the final document, Circular 8/94 (DfE 1994).)

- Policies should provide for the punishment of bad behaviour and encourage good behaviour.
- Policies should be specific to the school and/or classroom situation (Annex to DfE 1994).
- Rules should be kept to the minimum that is necessary to ensure good behaviour.
- The reasons for each rule should be clarified.
- Wherever possible, rules should be expressed in positive, constructive terms, although it should be absolutely clear what pupils are NOT allowed to do.

I suggest that these characteristics should also underpin the 'transactions' between teachers and pupils. Such characteristics, if employed, will go a long way in maintaining the dignity or self-esteem of both teacher and pupil. Basic principles such as those above assist in maintaining a balanced view of the politics, principles and practicalities of behaviour existing within the educational settings (Gribble 1993).

A dogged entrenchment during classroom transactions by either teacher or pupil may cause tensions to arise in the learning situation. This could detract from the educational aspects of the teaching and learning environment, often at the cost of the compliant or 'good' pupil. Charlton and David (1993) suggest that compromise, through negotiation between pupil and teacher, will need to take place in lessons for learning outcomes to be achieved. The 'tensions' described are often referred to by teachers as stress.

Rogers (1990) reported that disruptive pupil behaviour was the greatest cause of stress in the classroom. In their transactions, teachers should actively seek to develop approaches that attempt to prevent and alleviate such stress factors. Teachers employing such approaches will improve educational outcomes and their relationship with pupils.

In a report for the Department for Education and Employment (Daniels *et al.* 1998) pupils described 'good staff' as those who exhibited the following characteristics:

- 'Teachers who understand you and take an interest in you';
- 'After you have finished your work they ask how you are';
- 'They socialize with us (at school)';
- 'You get to like them (as people)'.

During my own teaching career, a much-improved SEBD male pupil once commented to me that the good ones (teachers) are:

'. . . polite and treat you with respect. If a teacher is in a foul mood or shouting at you, you do the same back.'

Daniels *et al.* (1998) suggested that 'staff must live by an agreed policy and desired values'. Schools where staff exhibit the above attitudes in their transactions with pupils, with an agreed school behavioural policy to support them, will be the most successful in delivering high-quality education and social values to their students. In a study by Cole *et al.* (1998), staff observed by pupils as managing classroom behaviour with effective 'transactions' exhibited the following characteristics. Staff are:

- 'confident yet have humility';
- 'genuine';
- 'able to develop warm relationships with pupils';
- 'listeners';
- 'able to exhibit care and understanding';
- 'able to receive and give appropriate physical contact to good effect'.

When you consider this list of attributes of the 'good' teacher obtained from SEBD pupils it makes you realize the burden of responsibility placed upon us. Teachers must accept that their transactions wield enormous power and influence upon very vulnerable and impressionable pupils.

Developing effective transactions

Research by Davie (1993) stated that there are some distinct approaches that can be employed in developing effective transactions with pupils. Theoretical models based upon psychological theory are often used to increase our understanding of pupil behaviour and the influences upon it.

The continuum of psychological theory helps me to understand the sources of some of these approaches. Behaviourism is a psychological approach that concentrates exclusively on observing, measuring and modifying behaviour. At the other end of the continuum are

117

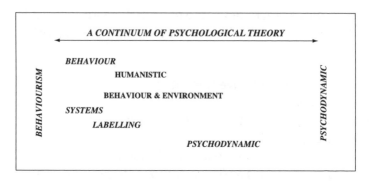

Figure 6.1 A continuum of psychological theory.

'psychodynamic' approaches. The latter are approaches based upon studies into the interaction of the emotional and motivational forces that affect behaviour and mental states, especially on a subconscious level.

The method best suited to behaviour-management transactions in classrooms and schools is still very much open to debate. Having a basic knowledge of those that can be employed may give some confidence and insight and help the reader in forming their own opinions as to which approach might best suit *their* situation. There appear to be research 'clusters' in the literature which form the basis of three theoretical models:

Skinnerian Behaviourism
This is a 'behaviourist' approach, rooted in the understanding of 'stimulus–response'. Such approaches have formed the basis for experiments to elicit desired behaviours in human beings and animals by ignoring unwanted behaviours and rewarding desired behaviours.

Freudian Psychoanalysis
This is a 'subject-centred' approach, historically used by Child and Adolescent Mental Health Teams. The results are derived from in-depth analysis of individual therapy sessions with clients. The approach requires cooperation and a great deal of time.

Rogerian Counselling
An approach based upon the work of the American Carl Rogers (1980). Rogers was a psychotherapist who developed the concept of 'counselling'. This is a 'self-concept' theory which allows the subject to come to an understanding of self through empathy.

The psychological model best suited to the developing of positive classroom transactions is open to debate. An informed, eclectic approach suited to the personality of the teacher and the environment they find themselves in with their pupils is probably the most pragmatic solution.

Kolvin (1981) in the Newcastle Study *Help Starts Here*, evaluated the effectiveness of the three theories in pupil transactions. He came to the conclusion that there was no clear forerunner in the methodologies, but found that in certain cases the very fact that pupils were referred for 'special treatment' had a positive effect upon their behaviour, no matter what that treatment was.

Kolvin also found that when teachers offer direct advice to their pupils this can be more effective than the involving of professionals external to the school. Kolvin recommends an 'eclectic' open-minded approach as being the best basis for the development of classroom-based interventions. Rayner (1998), in his analysis of the education of SEBD pupils, suggests that it is an eclectic 'pedagogy' that is the 'key' in managing classroom behaviour.

Further, Topping (1983) found that the more expensive interventions were not necessarily the more effective, and that there appeared to be a 66 per cent 'spontaneous remission' rate in populations of severely disruptive adolescents. Remission reportedly occurred no matter what type of intervention was undertaken. This is a view currently held with some scepticism (Grey *et al.* 1994). Topping compares the success rates of various support programmes to the phenomenon of spontaneous remission. Pragmatically and sensibly, Topping suggests that the *identification* of the source of problematic behaviour is the first step towards engineering a resolution. If teachers have the opportunity, they might take cognizance of this and attempt to observe pupil behaviour in context and record the emotions exhibited in order to understand the resulting behaviour. Such observation exercises by teachers are increasingly being employed in schools in the development of effective classroom-based transactions.

Eclectic, pragmatic approaches

In developing an eclectic, pragmatic approach to the transactions involved in managing classroom behaviour, Rogers (1990) based his work upon that of Kounin (1977). Kounin's central focus was that good classroom behaviour depends on effective learning management.

Kounin stated that the transactions between teacher and pupil need to be considered in terms of:

- pace
- transitions
- alerting
- individual accountability.

Transactions developed in this manner are intended to create and maintain a classroom atmosphere conducive to learning. By keeping pupils busily and happily engaged, behaviour problems are reduced to a minimum. In achieving this, teachers should be aware that they need to deal with the entire class – various sub-groups and individual students – often all at the same time!

According to Kounin, teachers need to be aware that they must learn to:

- know what is happening in every area of the classroom at all times and communicate that to pupils;
- be able to deal with more than one issue at a time;
- ensure the smooth transition from one activity to another;
- maintain group focus through alerting accountability;
- overcome student boredom, emphasizing progress, challenge and variety.

Kounin suggested some useful ideas for the promoting of effective teacher/pupil transaction:

The ripple effect

When teachers correct misbehaviour in one student, it often produces a 'ripple effect' in other pupils.
Examples:

'Good, I see that many of you are almost finished.'
'I see a few pupils who may have to stay in after class to finish.'

This transaction is more powerful in the primary sector. In the secondary sector the success of such transactions depends upon the popularity of the teacher.

With-it-ness

Kounin terms the awareness of what is transpiring in all parts of the classroom as 'with-it-ness'. If this trait is communicated by a teacher to their pupils, often more by body language than by voice, pupils are less likely to misbehave.
Example:
A teacher fully aware of what is going on in their classroom will immediately call to account the right culprit following a minor disruption. Pupils will perceive that the teacher is 'with it'.

Overlapping

Kounin terms the ability to attend to two issues at the same time as 'overlapping'.

Example:

A teacher is with a small group and notices that two students are playing cards instead of doing their assignment. The teacher could correct this by either:

i. Stopping the small-group activity, walking over to the card players and getting them back on-task, and then attempting to re-establish the activity;

or

ii. Having the small group continue while addressing the card players from a distance and then monitoring the students at their desks.

As you can see, the second approach involves over-lapping. Overlapping loses its effectiveness if the teacher does not also demonstrate 'with-it-ness'. If students working independently know that the teacher is aware of them and able to deal with them, they are more likely to remain on-task.

Movement

Kounin's research also revealed an important relationship between student behaviour and *movement* within and between lessons. He did not mean the physical movement of students or teachers. Instead he referred to the pacing, momentum and transitions.

Teachers' ability to move smoothly from one activity to the next, and to maintain momentum within an activity have a great deal to do with their effectiveness in controlling behaviour in the classroom. In smooth transitions, student attention is turned easily from one activity to another, thus keeping their attention on the task in hand.

Such advice is helpful to all teachers in their transaction planning. However, there are other processes which can be hijacked by pupils and teachers, sometimes for their own ends. Such processes include 'assertive discipline techniques', when employed inappropriately by teachers or pupils.

I applaud Kounin's theory and the programme. However, if not appropriately managed, it is possible for pupils to run up the tariff from 'name on the board' to 'yellow card' to 'red card'. I have heard from senior managers of cases where staff have managed the process in order to escalate situations, potentially leading to mass exclusions. Such outcomes should not arise when the aim is to include pupils and manage behaviour effectively.

The missing element in many transactions is empathy. All planned procedures need to be applied by teachers in an understanding and pragmatic manner. This manner should include recognition of Kounin's pedagogical principles in maintaining a balanced, rational educational environment.

Maintaining balance

I propose that every suggestion and theory for effective classroom transactions requires:

- adaptation to specific circumstances;
- constant evaluation and monitoring;
- a sustained team effort over a long period of time;
- reference to politics, policy and pragmatism.

In order to maintain a balanced, rational educational environment, it is crucial to consider lesson flow. The aim should be to promote a framework that maintains teachers' dignity and pupils' self-esteem. See Figure 6.2 below.

Cole *et al.* (1998) recognized that in planning for transactions (for SEBD pupils) teachers and schools could avoid deviance-inducing boredom, provide challenges and offer chances for relationship-building by balancing the relationship between:

- *Population*: Pupils, in sufficient numbers to permit a broad curriculum and allow for selection and group dynamics, and parents, whose support has been won by the reaching out to them in their community by staff through sustained effort.

Figure 6.2 Balancing classroom transactions.

- *People*: Pedagogues led by strong senior-management teams and supported by an empathetic, committed staff.
- *Provision*: Policies which are comprehensive on education, behaviour and care and that are practised, monitored and reviewed regularly. And, programmes that are differentiated, based upon strengths that build self-esteem through achievement and lead to normal goals.
- *Place*: A physical environment which is welcoming and sufficient for its use, is part of the community and has effective transport links to pupils' homes.

Another factor in maintaining a 'balance' in pupil/teacher transaction is establishing an 'ethos' which encourages a culture of solution-focused discussion rather than blame. This ethos should be built around the values and principles promoted by the institution and supported, responsibly, by the staff. This ethos is best described by Pearce (1989) when he suggests that in managing children's behaviour they require an environment that promotes the '6Cs':

> *'Constantly, Communicate, Clearly with Consistency, Conviction and Care.'*

Such a sensible yet simple mantra assists me in maintaining my 'multi-tasking' focus when working to maintain lesson flow. It also assists me in promoting desired behaviours in my teacher/pupil transactions:

- *Constant*: Am I giving a constant, strong impression that I am the 'authority' in 'authority'?

or

Am I 'moody' and unpredictable in my transactions? Do I 'telegraph' to pupils my insecurity and un-certainty in my transactions with them?

- *Communication*: Am I communicating to pupils the behaviours that are required and the outcomes for compliance and non-compliance?

or

Am I erratic, continually 'moving the goalposts' with-out any apparent logic?

- *Clearly*: Is my behavioural message clear? Have I explained why it is necessary to employ certain beha-viours rather than others? Have I been explicit in explaining which behaviours, spending time to clearly illustrate what is required to a variety of pupils with different emotional, conduct and learning behaviours?

or

Am I 'woolly' and unpredictable?

- *Consistent*: Am I being consistent in my approach? Do I 'follow-up' and follow through? Do I keep my promises? Can pupils rely upon my personality being the same? Will I be their 'sheet anchor in a storm'?

or

Does my personality continually vacillate and create a state of tension?

- *Conviction*: Do I live what I am promoting in terms of behaviour? Do I have a measured 'least intrusive–most intrusive' response to pupil behaviour in my transactions?

or

Do I tell pupils to 'do as I say, don't do as I do'?
- *Care*: Above all, do the behaviours that I am promoting in my transactions ensure that pupils feel safe, understood and happy? Are my working practices safe?

or

Is my pedagogical style lacking in any thought or plan, verging on the irresponsible?

I am eternally grateful to Dr John Pearce for this 'mantra'. It provides me with a personal, rapid, self-reflection tool that I can carry around in my head. It also provides a personal, mental trigger that enables me to 'engage brain before opening mouth'. In this way I am able to gauge where I am in Kounin's multidimensional, multi-tasking environment. I consciously manage my transactions with different pupils at different levels of compliance or non-compliance to the primary behaviour.

Another aspect of this fluid mental state that the teacher will need to adapt is the ability to 'relax' into the transaction process.

Health check

At this point you may be thinking that you are never going to be able to assimilate all this information. I remember what it was like learning to drive. I learned late. I am also left-handed and cross-lateral. Driving did not come easy, but I did it! You may think that you can never remember all the above – then don't try. Take on board that which will help you. Remember to:

- self-reflect in your quieter moments
- make planning notes
- script situations
- practise your teaching style
- discuss with colleagues to help improve your peda-gogical style.

Remember also that it is impossible to learn everything. There is always someone with a better idea and there is always a pupil or group of pupils who will challenge you and your beliefs. This is what makes the job stimulating.

It is very hard to teach in some of today's classrooms; isolation and lack of support may compound already difficult situations. Look for solutions and overcome self-doubt and blame by talking to others. Even in the darkest, most challenging periods of my career, I have been fortunate in always finding someone to listen. Keep your interests, keep healthy. 'Make time for you' was one of the best pieces of advice given to me by a deputy headteacher when I was a single person working in a residential secure unit. How right he was.

Least intrusive to most intrusive

As mentioned above, in the section on 'Maintaining Balance' in transactions, I have found that the concept of 'knowing where I am going' is an important con-sideration. It helps me both in the classroom and also with my planning. This concept is not new and came home strongly to me following a lecture by Dr John Robertson many years ago. It clarified for me what I was achieving and, often, not achieving in my transactions with pupils.

I already knew that many of the interactions I employed were successful and useful but this concept showed me, after many years as a teacher, where I was going. More importantly this process showed me where I could be going when employing appropriate 'transactions' with pupils. I hope that you will find it useful.

I include here a hierarchy of 'least intrusive to most intrusive' behaviours (Fig. 6.3). This is taken from Smith and Laslett (1993) who postulated that the 'disruptive teacher', as mentioned in Chapter 4, could minimize the amount of disruptive 'on-the-surface' or observable classroom behaviours by employing a hierarchy of planned, teacher behaviours. These ideas are far from new and I am astounded that this work was never included in my college course. Much of it was based upon the work of Redl and Wineman (1952). Such a consideration of behavioural transactions would have saved me from making many inappropriate mistakes in my dealings with pupils. The process, based upon pupils' reactions to stressful events, is designed to:

- change behaviour
- enhance self-esteem
- reduce anxiety
- expand understanding and insight into their own and others' behaviour and feelings (empathy).

Planned ignoring:
'Pretended' lack of awareness of undesirable behaviour. This should be
linked to positive attention to work at hand.

Signal interference:
Making eye contact or another signal to block further misbehaviour,
at the same time ensuring that the signal has been received.

Proximity control:
Teacher moves closer to the pupil and is linked with 'interest boosting'.

Interest boosting:
Specific intervention, such as marking and demonstration or modification
of the task.

Hurdle help:
Lessons are a 'hurdle' to learning. The teacher provides support to
overcome the 'hurdle'.

Tension decontamination through humour:
Confrontations between pupil and teacher may be relieved by a comment
or joke showing the funny side of the situation.

Hypodermic affection:
An injection of praise or 'affection'

Direct appeal:
Appeal to the pupil's sense of values: 'Do you really think I'm being unfair?'

Restructuring:
Change of activity.

Figure 6.3 Hierarchy of teacher behaviour for 'on surface behaviour'.

Redl and Wineman felt that it was helpful for students to see the connection between their feelings and behaviour. Pupils who show emotional and social maturity can say 'yes' to their feelings but 'no' to improper behaviour in expressing their feelings. We sometimes refer to this as 'pupils who cross the line'. This basic concept of supporting feelings but not the behaviour is frequently lost in the classroom transaction, as the teacher struggles to guide and teach pupils in crisis.

It would appear that these ideas underpin much of Dr Bill Rogers' and Dr John Robertson's work in the area of behaviour management in schools. These ideas can by utilized through the development of a stepped approach, a set of ongoing, learned teacher skills, managed within a framework of respect.

To make sense of the 'steps', I have drawn up a stepped approach (Gribble 1993b) to clarify the process – see Figure 6.4.

I found that developing clear steps of intervention as an aspect of my transactions with pupils helped me to develop more skills. I deduced that the more steps of intervention I included, the more opportunities there would be for pupils to conform to the desired classroom behaviours.

This is a naïve concept but it does help. It has also prevented me from racing up the hierarchy and taking a 'cannon to shoot a sparrow'. I have become much more rational and confident in my transactions. I now reason that the more I keep my behaviours in the 'white' area, the more likely it will be that pupils will remain on-task and that I will not be a 'disruptive' teacher.

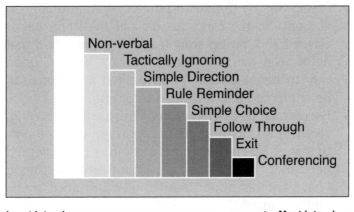

Least intrusive ──────────────────────────────▶ Most intrusive

Figure 6.4 A stepped approach: a set of ongoing, learnt teacher transactions, managed within a framework of respect.

As I use this approach and read more, I understand that I am balancing teacher attitude with skill acquisition. The more skills I acquire the more confident I become in my transactions and, in turn, my attitude improves. This has the effect of improving my relationships with pupils, and develops an 'upward spiral' mentioned by Cooper and Upton (1990).

A brief explanation of the steps follows:

Non-verbal

These are teacher behaviours that do not require the voice to be used. Examples are as follows:

- *Positioning*: By positioning myself as an authority, in authority in the class, standing at the front, hands clasped and gazing around at the pupils, I find that noise level naturally comes down. This is a good way to begin a lesson, and desired behaviour can be reinforced and rewarded by saying, 'Thank you'.
- *Eye contact*: By catching a pupil's eye and employing, very briefly, an appropriate expression directed only to that pupil, I will often get a glimmer of the desired behaviour. At that point, without embarrassment, I have another opportunity to give a positive 'metaphorical smartie'.
- *Non-verbal acknowledgement*: The use of simple hand gestures and facial expressions can re-enforce pupils' use of correct behaviours. A silent thank you, a smile, 'thumbs up' signal or OK sign are what I mean here. Similarly, this could be a frown, thumbs down or a pained expression; one that acknowledges that you have observed inappropriate behaviour. The teacher should consciously employ such acknowledgement throughout the lesson and increase those in type and range as their skills develop. Practising these gestures will show pupils you are 'with it', fully aware of the atmosphere in the classroom and will assist you in keeping pupils on-task without teacher interruption.

Tactically ignoring

This behaviour is employed by a teacher when the flow of the lesson is more important than inappropriate pupil behaviour. However, this is a 'tactical' approach and it may be necessary at a later point in the lesson to call a pupil to account for their behaviour(s). Inappropriate low-level behaviour such as 'passing wind', low-level swearing, belching or chair swinging must be followed up at some point. Not to do so gives the impression that the behaviour is acceptable.

Tactically ignoring a 'secondary behaviour' in order to concentrate on a 'primary' behaviour is an immensely useful teacher skill that I wish I had been taught at the outset. Repeating the primary request and tactically ignoring the behavioural 'display' put up a pupil or pupils is a powerful tool in keeping the 'flow'. Harry Enfield's comedy sketch character Kevin is a superb exponent of 'secondary behaviour', whose response is often:

'Fink I'm bovvered?'

Smith and Laslett's (1993) ideas of 'Tension decontamination through humour' involve tactical ignoring behavioural techniques. Many teachers employ this transaction type with great effect. I am continually amazed by the teachers I have observed using it; some can be so inventive, even in times of high tension. For example, in blocking inappropriate comments such as:

'You're stupid Sir!'

A mathematics teacher from Nottingham replied:

'Ah, but how do you know?'

An army-trained teacher, when called a b****** by a pupil, responded with:

'I think I have some certification somewhere to disprove your theory!'

My PE teacher at school, following an angry outburst from a pupil who had not brought the required kit, responded with:

'I tell you what, you come back when you're nice!'

I often use a phrase which helps redirect the lesson flow following an outburst. For example, a pupil saying loudly that:

*'This work is c***!'*

will get the response:

'Be that as it may . . .'

If you try to use this approach, and I know you will, it is likely you will overuse 'Be that as it may'. It works so well! I received a telephone call from a head of science to say the same; they kindly suggested an alternative:

'This is stupid!'
'That may be true!'

Such phrases should be collected and produced in a book on 'tips for teachers'! Their use promotes the successful regaining of lesson focus, maintains the dignity of both pupil and teacher, and demonstrates that you are 'with-it' (Kounin 1977).

Simple direction

Diffusion techniques tie in with these stransaction strategies. To minimize disruption, a hand gesture that non-verbally and privately 'calls' a pupil across the classroom can often have the desired effect of getting a pupil or pupils back on task. It allows a private discourse to take place that re-aligns behaviour quickly and maintain the flow of the lesson. Another method I have seen demonstrated is 'stating the obvious'. This is where a teacher reinforces the desired behaviour by framing it with a one-word question, such as:

'Working?'
'Talking?'
'Work-related?'
'Listening?'

This will not always work and may be seen as a hierarchy within a hierarchy in attempting to refocus behaviour onto the 'primary' behaviour.

It is often necessary to employ both short- and long-term strategies to direct behaviour, with patience. Often pupils won't always 'step into line'. One idea might be to have a 'behaviour book' in which incidents are recorded – pointing at the book and to the pupil may give a clear 'direction' that if the behaviour continues it will be noted, with follow up at a later date (Wolfendale 1992).

Rule reminder

This stage is a difficult one if classroom rules and routines have not been established. Establishing, reinforcing and invoking agreed consequences makes this level of intervention the richest and most involved step. It is one that I do not really want to go beyond, and with most pupils I won't need to. This is because I have taken time to establish rules and routines within a 'Rights and Responsibility' framework. The messages given within this framework are:

Compliance = Opportunity
Rights + Responsibilities = Rule

The final section of this chapter will look at the simple development of rules in more detail.

Simple choice

After exhausting the above, some pupils will require a more intrusive approach. Returning to the 'behaviour book', I might have to say,

'Unfortunately, your behaviour is such that you have made me record your name in the book.'

Such a statement implies choice.

'It was not me, the teacher, doing something to you; it was you, the pupil, causing it to happen.'

The dignity and self-esteem of both teacher and pupil will be maintained if the message is extended by saying:

'You're wonderful but what you're doing is totally unacceptable and has caused this to happen.'

The teacher can maintain a dialogue in such situations, pointing out that a pupil or pupils can choose to be different. The teacher also has an opportunity to say what pupils have to do to achieve a compliant state and also what they are missing by following their current course of action. Of course you may still get 'Fink I'm bovvered?!'

Following through

This is the application of agreed consequences. It ensures that misdemeanours are followed up quickly, fairly and within agreed, pre-planned guidelines. It is perhaps the most important step for the repeat offender. It gives the clear message that:

'You caused this to happen. It was agreed. If I didn't do this I would be letting you down as it would be giving you the wrong message.'

Employing the use of a 'behaviour book' to develop appropriate consequences during periods of 'calm' rather than 'high emotion' is also very useful and gives an opportunity to check sanctions out with colleagues to ensure they are viable and legal!

Exit

There may come a time when you need to remove a pupil from class. Developing strategies to achieve this in advance of needing them can save disruptive situations from escalating further and make for a safer environment.

Walking away, gesturing for a pupil to follow and at the same time ignoring the secondary behaviours is one strategy. Sending a runner to another member of staff is moving up a notch. Pressing 'panic' buttons, calling pagers, using telephones and even contacting the police are going to extremes, but you may need to go this far in giving pupils clear messages regarding acceptable and unacceptable classroom behaviour. If you have pre-planned your strategy and have agreed it with colleagues, it is less likely that you will need to employ it.

Conferencing

Continual low-level attrition or extremes of behaviour, resulting in 'Exit' will require external assistance. You will need to plan, with the pupil and their carer, to develop strategies that assist the pupil's re-integration into the classroom. Planning for re-entry is vital after any exclusion. To leave this aspect to chance will 'emotion-ally' exclude pupils. Unfortunately I have observed a school that employed this strategy to encourage non-school attendance.

There is one step that does not appear in my model because it exists between each of the steps:

Take-up time

One of the greatest behavioural skills that I have learned, as a teacher and in life, is that of giving an instruction, expecting compliance and leaving the recipient of the request/demand alone with it. Time and time again I find that pupils (and adults), if left for a moment to consider their options or just to allow a request/demand to 'sink in', will comply with a teacher's wishes. This skill has been termed by numerous writers in the field of behaviour management as 'take-up time'.

Take-up time demands nerve, skill and, above all, patience. Allowing pupils to choose their course of action and helping them to feel in control is very impor-tant when working with SEBD pupils. The teacher who falls into the trap (often set by the SEBD pupil) of saying:

'Well, if you don't do it now, I will stand next to you until it is done!'

might be in for a long wait, or worse, might invite confrontation and increased lesson disruption.

Rules

Bill Rogers (1990) advocated that in the development of rules practitioners employ the concept of '4Rs'. Simply put:

$$\frac{\text{Rights} + \text{Responsibility} = \text{Rule}}{\text{Recovery}}$$

Teachers, in establishing themselves as 'confident classroom leaders', will need to go through the following procedures. This process will need to be undertaken very early on, perhaps in the first meeting with a new class. Such procedures will require careful consideration and planning. Time spent on such activities will give you more time to teach. If there are pre-prescribed school rules, do not be put off. I would still recommend going through the procedures as an opportunity to explain how those rules were arrived at in order to gain some ownership. This is the danger with prescribed rules. If somebody says:

'Keep off the grass!'

the first thing I want to do is step on it to see what will happen. If nothing happens what is the point of the rule? However, if somebody says to me:

'Bill, keep off the grass because this is a site of scientific interest and we are trying to maintain the underlying archaeology.'

I'm in there – keeping other people off the grass too! I understand and respect the rule. Rules can be printed, published and put into 'pupil planners' but if they are not 'owned', understood or explained to pupils, carers, parents, teachers, school employees, governors and visitors to the school, they will fall into disuse.

Imposed rules promote arrogance in an institution. They imply that rules sometimes exist purely for the people who work there rather than the clients that the institution is set up to serve.

The process of 'rule-making' should underpin whole-school policy. It should be transparent and should support everybody's rights in the school context. The rule-making process should be open to regular review and be integral to the day-to-day procedures in improving life for everybody. It must be communicated outside the institution, with an explanation of how outsiders (parents and carers in particular) can contribute to the review process. This is most effective in the form of a 'Home-School Agreement'. Form tutors, heads of year or house heads should ensure that it is understood by *all* pupils, parents, carers and external agencies, prior to a pupil being admitted. This is a school's opportunity to say:

'When you come here (behaviourally) we expect you to do this.'
'We (as a school) guarantee that we will do this.'
'If these rules are infringed, this will happen.'
'Included in this document are ways in which you can contribute to the review process.'

Developing classroom rules

i. Through an explanation of the rights pertaining in a classroom or wider school context, pupils and teachers should first agree on what the classroom rights are. Bill Rogers (1990) suggests 'six key' areas that assist in focusing this explanation:

- communication
- learning
- movement
- problem-solving
- treatment
- safety.

ii. Following agreement upon each other's rights in the classroom in the above areas of focus, the discussion can then lead on to how to mutually respect these rights.

iii. The concept of responsibility is explored next. Pupils and teachers, through such discussions, will each learn that if they do not respect each other's rights, and are not responsible in the maintenance of those rights, then their own rights cannot be enjoyed.

iv. There should follow a discussion about the rules that need to be in place to ensure the maintenance of each other's rights. The discussion will need to cover how the rules work in the following 'transactions':

- pupil to pupil
- pupil to teacher
- teacher to pupil.

v. There should then be a discussion about the language one should employ in writing up the agreed rules and what happens when rights are impinged upon.
vi. The 'rules' are agreed and formally recorded.
vii. Rule infringement will now require discussion. Consequences of actions can be discussed at this point. This can lead to the formal development of consequences. I ask pupils to consider a 'least intrusive' to 'most intrusive' set of consequences. I do not employ that phraseology but I might ask:

> 'What if it was an accident?'
> 'What if they forgot?'
> 'What if it was deliberate?'
> 'What if they couldn't help it?'

viii. The recording of outcomes from these discussions should be in the form of a 'sliding scale' of agreed teacher intervention. This scale is known and planned in advance of it needing to be used.
ix. This complete process should result in three outcomes:

- An agreed set of rules;
- An agreed set of sanctions for non-compliance to the agreed rules;
- An agreed set of 'rewards' for compliant behaviour.

The word 'reward' might give practitioners a problem here but, for want of a better word, it is how classroom leaders acknowledge that pupils have complied. The message to pupils at this point is:

145

'Compliance = Opportunity'

x. The 'recovery' stage is how, following impinge-
ments upon others' rights, or rule infringement, the
situation is recovered or normalized. I find that a
good trigger in this discussion is:

'How do we fix things when they have gone wrong?'

The resulting discussions often reinforce my 'steps
of intervention'. Pupils will often say:

'Well if we're too difficult you might have to . . .
    take someone out.'
    call someone in.'
    ask parents to come to school.'
    set a detention.'

and even

ask their parents/guardians to sit next to them in
class!'

I undertook this exercise with a group of Year 9 pupils
(Year 3 in Scotland). We had established the rules and
précised language in writing them down. Upon the
pupils' return from an Easter vacation, I decided to revisit
these 'rules'. I explained my intention to the class and a
pupil said:

'You're not going through them all again are you?'

I said that I would be, to which he replied:

'We know 'em'
'You know your job don't you, eh?'
'It's your job to do us if we break 'em!'

I took this as a compliment because they had interna-lized the rules, and they had developed an ownership of them. Most important of all, they had sanctioned me to employ the agreed consequences!

I suggest that a similar process is undertaken to develop rules in the wider context of the school. I have found 'school councils' an excellent 'policy-making body' when formulating school-wide rules and in carry-ing the reasons for rules to the pupil population.

Protocols

It is important to reiterate here that in all transactions teachers will need to employ appropriate 'protocols' or ways of working. These protocols are 'peppered' throughout this book and supported by research.

Summary

Teachers need to employ the following protocols in their transactions:

- minimize embarrassment
- avoid arguing
- keep a sense of humour
- be consistent

- follow up good and inappropriate behaviour
- self-reflect
- practise 'take-up time'
- use wide support in planning
- remember 'It's only a job!'
- colleagues are the best resource.

Considered transactions in developing appropriate pedagogical styles will achieve success with most pupils but not all.

7 Conclusion

'. . . schools and other settings can be expected to solve most behaviour problems themselves but they cannot solve them all.' (Ofsted (2005)

For many children, their schooldays are not the happiest days of their lives. Increasingly, children and young people are becoming excluded, or exclude themselves from the process of state education in the United Kingdom (Parsons 1996).

Mainstream schools are increasingly being encouraged to include these same, disaffected children in their classrooms (Welsh Office 1999). There appears, however, to be too few opportunities for teachers to learn the skills that will enable them to cope with changes in pupil behaviour. Continuing changes in professional expectation by government and society also increase the pressures placed upon teachers.

At the end of the last millennium, the Elton Report (1989) concluded that teachers were not being 'beaten up' by disruptive and violent children. Rather they were being 'beaten down' by new initiatives and changes to the curriculum. At the beginning of this millennium, it seems reasonable to ask the question:

'How much of this reality has in fact really changed?'

More importantly, perhaps, is the related question of how this explanation, and others, can help teachers and pupils better manage classroom behaviour?

There are no panaceas by which inclusion in the education process for all children will be achieved. Neither does it appear to be desirable that mainstream schools attempt to educate *all* emotionally and behaviourally disturbed children (Daniels *et al.* 1998). There is, however, a real opportunity for schools to become places where a sense of *belonging* can be encouraged in most children, and acceptable behaviours can be taught by teachers and their colleagues. Moreover, I suggest that schools and teachers who adopt such a position will enhance pupils' achievement.

Managing behaviour and misbehaviour: a positive approach

Charlton and David (1993) argued that it is possible to manage some of the more extreme or challenging behaviour presented by pupils in the mainstream classroom. Much can be achieved by supportive teachers and by schools adopting a positive approach to behaviour management (see Gribble 1993).

Accepting this premise, and with the aim of developing a system to manage most pupils' behaviour in mainstream schooling, it is helpful, indeed perhaps necessary, to identify some important points regarding the management of pupil behaviour in the school context. These include:

- A recognition by schools of the influence of behaviour exhibited by adults on pupils who are connected in any way to the school.
- A realization by adults connected to the school that confrontational styles of behaviour management can produce adverse reactions in children.
- Observing children's behaviour in the classroom and in the wider context of the school assists adult understanding in planning behaviour management strategies. These strategies help pupils in the development of appropriate school-based behaviour.
- Listening to and consulting with children, parents, carers, colleagues and other agencies involved with the child at school can give everyone an opportunity to understand current behaviour patterns. This encourages personal responsibility.
- Recognizing that self-control in adults and pupils, and a consideration of the needs of others, gives everybody more time for individual learning.
- Pre-planned and agreed consequences are more effective and acceptable than punishment.

All parents and teachers need to accept that difficult and disobedient behaviours are part of normal child development. The dilemma for both carers and teachers is: which behaviours are just passing phases of 'naughtiness' and which behaviours, if left unchecked, are damaging to pupils and those around them. This dilemma has been epitomized by R. D. Laing (1970), one of the best-known psychiatrists of our modern times, who observed that:

> It is our duty to bring up our children to love, honour and obey us.
> If they don't, they must be punished,
> otherwise we would not be doing our duty.
> If they grow up to love, honour and obey us
> we have been blessed for bringing them up properly.
> If they grow up not to love, honour and obey us,
> either we have brought them up properly
> or we have not:
> If we have,
> there must be something the matter with them;
> if we have not,
> there must be something the matter with us!

In this insightful but simple text from Laing's book entitled *Knots* (1970) Laing presents the parent and teacher with the eternal, ganglionic question 'Is it me or is it them?' The emotional turmoil created by such questioning and the inherent dilemmas therein have been the source of much of mankind's philosophical deliberation. Learning that has been developed from this deliberation appears to form at least one aspect of a civilized society's formation of order and good citizenship.

The management of behaviour and the learning process appears all too often to be wrapped up in the 'us and them' question of 'blame'. Laing hints in his text that the way forward towards a resolution will need to be sought in the transaction, not in the people. Perhaps the people involved are just simply being human. Is it simply their behaviour rather than nature that requires some modification?

The way in which we can improve behaviour is very much down to how we develop the skills of inter-action between teacher and pupil. There is a need for these skills to be mutually understood, respected, taught or learned. It appears necessary, therefore, for those involved in the business of managing these trans-actions to, metaphorically, stand back and observe the continuing series of interpersonal relationships and, in some detail, attempt to understand the processes involved.

Self-reflection of this type is often difficult to achieve when you are close to the process. When you are already 'beaten down' by the daily 'give and take' of working with these difficulties or problem behaviours, such a position might be impossible without external, collegi-ate support. However, my thesis is that by adopting this position of self-reflection and observation in the development of the teaching and learning environment, teachers can begin to remove the need for blame. They can concentrate instead on how the process or trans-action can be improved. This should lead to successful and confident teacher behaviour and the development of collegiate, in-house strategies that assist pupils in the development of behaviours that enhance the teach-ing and learning process. Schools can develop strategies that improve their procedures and transactions and that ultimately create a more positive learning environment for all.

It is important to remember that each player has a role to play in this drama of social interaction and learning. Furthermore, it is important that each participant knows their place in this scenario and is encouraged to feel safe, secure and confident. This confidence will enhance the role of other players. Knowing the script, rehearsing scenes and preparing for the performance, in terms of behaviour management, are as important for professional development and whole-school planning for behaviour as they are for any other school activity.

The ultimate aim for school-based staff, in an ideal world, would be to teach all the adults involved in the school community their role in behavioural transactions. This training would provide a level of understanding that equips them with the emotional skills to respond appropriately and with confidence in most behavioural transactions. Thus, when involved in teacher and pupil behaviour transactions, we should know where we are going.

Schools making the difference

Education, or the teaching of our society's combined knowledge and beliefs, does make a difference to the prospects of pupils' careers (Coleman and Hendry 1990). However, there is an increasing number of conduits or routes down which the various forms of knowledge can travel to the pupil. As individuals, we will never control all these conduits. We cannot prevent some aspects of knowledge reaching and influencing our society's children, even though some of this knowledge may be faulty, biased and, at worst, damaging. Figure 7.1 looks at the variables that appear to influence student achievement. The variables are different for each child as are the conduits reaching them. Figure 7.1 illustrates clearly the areas those adults who work with children can influence.

It would appear futile and a waste of valuable time in school to attempt to influence certain 'unalterable' or 'hard to change' factors. These include individual differences which are relatively fixed or are features of family and home environment. As adults who work with pupils in school, however, it is necessary for us to understand the effect that these influences will have upon the individuals we teach. It is important that we are aware of when to compensate for adverse circumstances or individual difficulty by adjusting those areas that are 'alterable'.

Attempting to influence these factors and adapting according to the needs of the individuals in our schools will assist in creating a meaningful learning experience. Adults involved in the process of teaching and learning will be better equipped through this understanding when attempting to include more young people in the educational process. The consideration of alterable and unalterable states is similar to the development of personal construct or 'mindset', within an ecosystemic framework.

As teachers and carers, understanding and developing our skills will assist us in controlling and ultimately influencing some of the previously described conduits for

Within student	External to student
Desire to learn	Quality of curriculum
Strategies for learning	Quality of teaching
Learning style	
Alterable	**Alterable**
Skills (social coping)	Motivation of teacher
Prior content knowledge	Pedagogical knowledge
Self-efficacy	Subject knowledge
Helplessness (perceived or	Quality and type of evaluation
otherwise)	Quality of learning environment
	Quality of time given
	Use made of time allowed
Unalterable	**Unalterable**
Race (perception of race	
by others)	
Genetic potential	
Gender	
Hard to change	**Hard to change**
Disposition	Family income and resources
Birth order	Peer socioeconomic status
Health/diet	Family housing
Physical differences	Parents' schooling
IQ	Family mobility
EQ	Family siblings and extended
Disability category	family values
Personal history	Family History

Figure 7.1 Variables which influence student achievement (Howell 1998).

learning. This is particularly important when working with pupils in school. The above framework offers us the opportunity to understand and respond to behaviours that are the consequence of a wide variety of influences, and further to acknowledge that some influences on pupil behaviour and achievement are unalterable.

It is important to then concentrate on areas on which adults in the school context can exercise some positive influence. This seems to be the most appropriate and productive course of action for the practising teacher. As parents, carers and teachers it is also important to understand that, as adults, we have a duty of care to the pupils with whom we interact (Whitney 1993). Failure in that duty has grave implications for individuals, education and society. Understanding what our duties are in guiding pupils along the most appropriate conduits fundamental to both good teaching and good parenthood.

Applying a professional approach to behaviour management

Understanding the influences upon behaviour can lead us to conclude that behaviour is learned and that observed behaviour is based upon discernible choice. Choice appears fundamental in the process of managing behaviour. If we choose to be in control of our own behaviour and to channel it to improve our situation, and if we are successful, we are usually motivated to repeat those behaviours. If this motivation is nurtured or rewarded positively, again, the behaviour pattern may be repeated. As educationalists, an aspect of our role is to help our students to understand this process. It is important for pupils to understand that it is more desirable, even profitable, to work with others constructively.

As professionals in the school context, we should assist pupils in understanding that they can achieve more by being cooperative in their interpersonal relationships. Working in isolation does not always assist self-reflection. Observing and recording behaviour and subsequently analysing it is an important part of the process.

A helpful idea in developing this technique, taken from behavioural psychology, looks at behaviour in terms of an ABC approach: Antecedents, Behaviours and Consequences. This key construct can be used to help us to understand what it is that drives behaviour in both adults and pupils.

Wheldall and Merrett (1984) use this idea in their book *Positive Teaching* to help teachers develop a positive teaching style; a style of teaching that leaves the behaviour and the consequences of that behaviour firmly with the pupil. It should immediately be acknowledged that this requires great self-control on the part of the teacher. From day one of my teaching career, I have found it difficult, even undesirable, to 'control' pupils' behaviour. I have learned since that it is self-control that is the most important aspect of classroom management. Bill Rogers, in recent correspondence with me, referred to Aristotle's Nicomachean Ethics. Aristotle advised mankind not to forget that it is human to be painfully affected by anger and to find revenge sweet:

'Anyone can become angry – that is easy. But to be angry with the right person, to the right degree, at the right time for the right purpose, and in the right way – this is not easy.' (Aristotle 385–322 BC)

It would seem that choosing to be in control of one's own behaviour is the preferred state. Even when we are angry and to some extent are 'losing control', it is desirable to regain control of our emotions and often much more effective. This implies a clear understanding of the options open to us in a given context, in this case the classroom. A teacher or carer, if they are going to give clear messages, needs to exhibit self-control.

They are required to understand social context and to teach pupils to adopt different behaviours within various social settings. In order for pupils to get the most out of school life, teachers and carers need to assist them in developing and acquiring the necessary behaviours, skills and attitudes to adapt to various social contexts. The pupil who learns that different behaviour is required in different contexts is on the journey towards world citizenship. Throughout evolution, we see that it is this adaptability which causes an organism to thrive and be successful. The same appears to be true for the pupil in the context of the school.

Teachers will need to have a clear vision of what is required in terms of preferred practice in classrooms. Parents and carers will need a similar vision for life at home. This should be an aim for all teachers and parents. A *preferred practice* is the desired behaviour that one wishes to elicit or exhibit in a given context (Rogers 1995).

How often is this vision lost by us all in the daily grind? Through planning and considering the impact of our own behaviours upon others, we can work towards at least two important aspects of these preferred practices:

- The first preferred practice would be the ability to recover the situation.
- The second is a consistent methodology or process; planning in advance approaches that will consider the clear, consistent and positive messages we wish to give to children.

When applying a professional approach to managing behaviour, theoretical models are helpful in the planning of and the development of interventions. Which method is best-suited to behaviour management in classrooms and schools is very much open to debate. Theoretical models do, however, give direction when managing classroom behaviour. Knowledge of the different approaches gives confidence and insight. This insight leads to the development of eclectic approaches that suit individual and group need.

Maslow's concept of a hierarchy of needs is still useful in conceptualizing where a pupil is 'at' in terms of their emotional development (1954). McGuiness (1993) puts these ideas into a clear context when he develops his ideas of the 'Sociogenic effect', stating:

'Schools do not work in a vacuum, nor do staff work in a climate unaffected by the larger, different worlds within which we and our pupils live.'

Rayner (1998), in his analysis of the education of pupils with emotional and behaviour difficulties, also suggests that it is an eclectic pedagogy that is the key in managing classroom behaviour.

An example of one such practical, eclectic approach is that postulated by Cooper and Upton (1990). They utilized the theory associated with an ecosystemic model, an approach previously identified in this book as a strategic approach to planning intervention. Within this ecosystemic framework, problem behaviour is not seen as originating from within pupils but from within the interaction between pupils and the adults in the school context. The approach concentrates upon the process, not the 'us and them'.

When employing an ecosystemic approach in managing classroom and whole-school behaviour, the teacher (and any other adult in the school) uses personal constructs or perceptions set against the constructs of others in the social system. This involves the teacher in a degree of self-analysis. It creates opportunities to break cycles of behaviour that could otherwise become entrenched.

Another example of an eclectic approach, one of many, is that put forward by Bill Rogers (1994). His general model for school discipline and classroom management is described as a positive approach to managing behaviour. Roger's eclectic and pragmatic ideas, influenced by the work of Dreikurs *et al.* (1982) and Kounin (1977) reflect similar thinking found in Topping's early work (1983). Topping suggested that by merely concentrating on positive language, the adults who work with children in schools can make a positive difference to their exhibited behaviour. Topping concluded that children in an environment of positive language were, subsequently, more likely to reach a clear understanding of what is acceptable classroom behaviour.

The above ideas are being encapsulated by central government in guidance from the Department for Education and Skills. The Key Stage 3 National Strategy (DfES 2004a) tasks schools with undertaking joint training and policy-making events. These concentrate on managing pupil behaviour and on the encouragement of good attendance. Guidance in this process is offered by the QCA (2001). The key messages from these are very pertinent (see DfES 2003):

- Improvement in behaviour and attendance requires comprehensive whole-school actions; 'one-off' training sessions are unlikely to lead to embedded change.
- The behaviour and attendance strategy builds upon the existing range of school self-evaluation and improvement activities.
- *All* adults within the school community should become skilled and active in improving behaviour and attendance.
- Behaviour and attendance improvement starts with staff understanding the causal factors, and leads on to an appreciation of pupil needs.
- Improvements in behaviour and attendance will lead to an improvement not only in standards and inclusion but also in the quality of the day-to-day experiences for pupils and staff within schools.

It would appear that we are not just teachers of subjects, we are teachers of children. A common response to this is 'I wasn't trained to do that!'

SEBD and a positive response

In what many might perceive as an increasingly troubled society, children and young people with social, emotional and behavioural difficulties (SEBD) form the largest and fastest growing special needs group (Webb 1992; Parsons 1996). The *Education Act 1993* to some extent institutionalized the SEBD child by creating Pupil Referral Units where they could be educated off-site. The underlying factors, such as why there are a growing number of SEBD pupils in our society, do not appear to be successfully addressed. Nevertheless, the *Education Act 1996* and the *1997 Supplement* did go further than any other legislation in imposing a duty on schools and Local Education Authorities to include all pupils in the education process. As far as possible, this was to be in mainstream school settings. The process of planning, strategy formation and target setting are at the heart of this legislation.

The social inclusion government 'think tank' has at its policy core education and training as the vehicles for bringing back into our society disaffected and disengaged young people. 'New Start', Connexions and 'Youth Access' have been products of this drive. Youth Offender Teams and cross-county council agencies and departments see 'citizenship' and 'acceptable conduct in the community' as an aim of education.

Currently, interest and demands offer educationalists an opportunity to reflect on our present behaviour-management practices. This is generated largely by what appears to be a quest for an appropriate, cost-effective education system by central government. It is also the case that recent government guidance is increasingly taking a similar line, reflecting the attempt to identify and disseminate good practice (see, for example, Daniels *et al.* 1998; QCA/DfEE 1999; DfES Key Stage 3 Strategy 2003).

Planning for and developing an appropriate curriculum appears to be the key to effective classroom management. This should be based upon the emotional and academic needs of pupils (Greenhalgh 1994).

Planning for behaviour by Local Education Authorities (LEAs) has been conducted through the framework of an LEA Behaviour Support Plan. The national press has reported that, statistically, this has reduced the need to permanently exclude pupils. Do the statistics reflect the reality? An LEA model of SEBD support is proposed in Appendix 1.

The QCA produced a useful document in their 'Supporting School Improvement' series entitled *Emotional and Behavioural Development* (2001) to assist schools in the planning process.

As a foundation for effective education, a positive 'stepped' management approach can be effective for pupils experiencing behavioural difficulties. Schools can actively and directly help pupils experiencing difficulty or failure to regain their self-respect and, above all, their dignity. Within a supportive education system, pupils can develop self-esteem and enter society as 'full citizens'.

One example of a specific class-based approach reflecting this is 'Circle Time' (Mosley 1999). This is a method for securing the empowerment of children and young people as an aid in helping them understand their behaviour and the behaviour of others. Mosley described the development of self-esteem and self-discipline as an essential element in this process. The approach is aimed at developing a system of classroom and school behaviour management that nurtures direct 'involvement' and 'ownership' of the process by pupils, while overlapping with other areas of learning activity within the classroom.

An indication of the importance of an understanding of self-esteem and self-discipline as an aspect of the protocols required in developing such a system of positive behaviour management is also presented by Bill Rogers in his book *Behaviour Management* (1995). A protocol, in this sense, is a term used to describe one or more principles that we agree to observe as teachers in school, working with both colleagues and pupils. Rogers explores this further in his 2002 work *I Get By With a Little Help*.

Following such principles makes us more consistent in our interaction with our pupils. Instead of relying on our personality or power-base, we can genuinely and humanely maintain good relationships in the classroom and guide pupils towards self-controlled behaviour. Rogers (1998) has referred to these protocols as 'preferred practices'. A balanced observation of such protocols helps maintain the dignity of teacher/adult and pupil/child relationships or transactions (see Farrell 1995; Mosley 1999).

It is important to develop 'mutual respect' between the participants involved in any teaching and learning at a whole-school level. The creation of a school behaviour-management policy is a statutory requirement. An example of a proposed school behaviour policy is included in Appendix 2. The DfE Circulars on Pupils with Problems, commonly referred to as the' six pack' (1994), strongly recommended that successful whole-school policies for behaviour management contain the following features:

- Be simple and straightforward, and be based on a clear and defensible set of principles or values.
- Mutual respect is a useful starting point. (This phrase was used in the guidance document, DfE 1993, *Pupils with Problems*, but did not appear in the final guidance – Circular 8/94 which, I believe, is a sad omission.)
- Provide for the punishment of bad behaviour and encourage good behaviour.
- Be specific to the school and/or classroom situation (Annex DfE Circular 8/94, 1994).
- Rules should be kept to the minimum necessary to ensure good behaviour.
- The reasons for each rule should be clear.
- Wherever possible rules should be expressed in positive, constructive terms, although it should be absolutely clear what pupils are not allowed to do.

In order to maintain the dignity of both teacher and pupil, it is important to maintain a balanced view of the politics, principles and practicalities of the educational settings in which sets of behaviour are exhibited (Gribble 1993b). These aspects of human interaction are necessary considerations, especially in the context of the school. They are equally important considerations in the development and implementation of a behaviour-management policy. It is almost as simple as saying 'get real' if you want it to actually 'work'.

It is important not to lose sight of the effect that the school itself will have on the behaviour-management structures in school. The organization and structure of it will greatly affect the ethos and success of behaviour management. All the theoretical knowledge and rhetoric available, focused upon a single issue or problem, will not overcome a particular set of attitudes, particularly attitudes perpetuated by senior management. The politics of the social context need to be understood. Changing the attitudes of fellow professionals may be very difficult but not insurmountable if the parameters are known and the political system that distributes the power is understood.

Postman and Weingartner (1976) suggested that school teachers have a responsibility to provide the young with a 'What is it good for?' perspective on their own society's rule-making and discipline procedures. Sometimes, discipline, in today's society, is considered to be a dirty word. Discipline, like most words in our language, has many connotations. In Latin, *disciplina* means 'teaching' in the school context. Thus, in school it should refer to self-control, order, and the opportunity to teach, rather than correction or punishment. This concept lies at the heart of the perspective on behaviour management that is presented throughout this book. Furthermore, establishing appropriate relationships, agreeing rights and demarcating responsibilities are all perceived as essential features of effective discipline. While boundaries and firmness are aspects of developing a framework for discipline, so is an emphasis upon flexibility, genuineness and regard for pupils by the teacher.

Ensuring authority, as an exercise, may be likened to commanding respect. It is a commodity that is earned rather than obtained by demand. A good manager will exercise discipline and control in such a way that those who are managed are part of the process which sees respect grow.

A dogged entrenchment during classroom transactions, either by the teacher or the pupil, inevitably results in confrontation. This causes tension in the learning situation (Parsons and Howlett 1996) and directly affects the relationships between pupils and teachers. It also impacts upon learning performance. Compromise, if possible by negotiation, is a more preferred course of action (Charlton and David 1993).

Compromise should not be a win or lose transaction but should be based upon prior, agreed and understood principles. This realization by the adults involved in the teaching–learning relationship is what Rogers (1995) calls preferred practice, as referred to above.

Preferred practices, principles or protocols are established and agreed by those affected by them. It is essential that principles are developed in consultation with the protagonists who will use them, especially in the school context.

Conclusion

Coping with personal stress and reaching a position where self-control is achieved by both teacher and pupil underpins what has earlier been termed a 'positive approach' to classroom behaviour management (Rogers 2002). This eclectic approach does not seek to *own* a student's behaviour but instead seeks to assist the student in owning their own behaviour, whilst at the same time giving the guarantee that the teacher will be in full control of this and their behaviour.

Maintaining dignity in the classroom requires a balance between what is politic, what is agreed in principle and what can be done immediately, in specifically pragmatic terms. This understanding gives a new confidence and a feeling of self-worth to teachers which should make the classroom a more effective and enjoyable place to be.

Adopting a decisive teaching style that establishes authority and conveys regard is crucial. Adults in the school context can learn to respect students, even if they do not like them!

Summary

- Adults in school can manage personal stress and develop self-control in themselves and their students.
- There needs to be an open culture which recognizes, analyses, records and evaluates behaviour in a management framework.
- An achievable template for such a culture is an eclectic approach.
- Corporate and collegiate planning is crucial.

Appendix 1: A proposed LEA model of SEBD support. A stepped-approach model of behaviour support

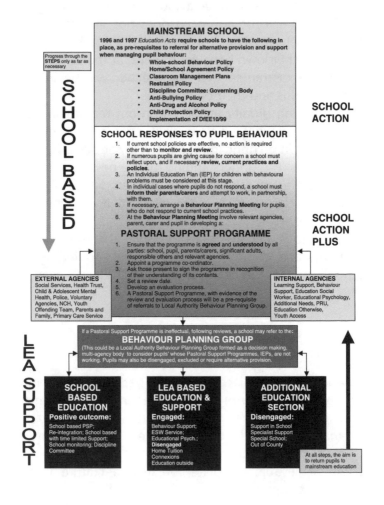

MAINSTREAM SCHOOL

1996 and 1997 *Education Acts* require schools to have the following in place, as pre-requisites to referral for alternative provision and support when managing pupil behaviour:
- Whole-school Behaviour Policy
- Home/School Agreement Policy
- Classroom Management Plans
- Restraint Policy
- Discipline Committee: Governing Body
- Anti-Bullying Policy
- Anti-Drug and Alcohol Policy
- Child Protection Policy
- Implementation of DfEE10/99

Progress through the STEPS only as far as necessary

SCHOOL ACTION

SCHOOL RESPONSES TO PUPIL BEHAVIOUR

1. If current school policies are effective, no action is required other than to **monitor and review**.
2. If numerous pupils are giving cause for concern a school must reflect upon, and if necessary **review, current practices and policies**.
3. An Individual Education Plan (IEP) for children with behavioural problems must be considered at this stage.
4. In individual cases where pupils do not respond, a school must **inform their parents/carers** and attempt to work, in partnership, with them.
5. If necessary, arrange a **Behaviour Planning Meeting** for pupils who do not respond to current school practices.
6. At the **Behaviour Planning Meeting** involve relevant agencies, parent, carer and pupil in developing a:

PASTORAL SUPPORT PROGRAMME

1. Ensure that the programme is **agreed** and **understood** by all parties: school, pupil, parents/carers, significant adults, responsible others and relevant agencies.
2. Appoint a programme co-ordinator.
3. Ask those present to sign the programme in recognition of their understanding of its contents.
4. Set a review date.
5. Develop an evaluation process.
6. A Pastoral Support Programme, with evidence of the review and evaluation process will be a pre-requisite of referrals to Local Authority Behaviour Planning Group.

SCHOOL ACTION PLUS

EXTERNAL AGENCIES
Social Services, Health Trust, Child & Adolescent Mental Health, Police, Voluntary Agencies, NCH, Youth Offending Team, Parents and Family, Primary Care Service

INTERNAL AGENCIES
Learning Support, Behaviour Support, Education Social Worker, Educational Psychology, Additional Needs, PRU, Education Otherwise, Youth Access

SCHOOL BASED

LEA SUPPORT

If a Pastoral Support Programme is ineffectual, following reviews, a school may refer to the:
BEHAVIOUR PLANNING GROUP
(This could be a Local Authority Behaviour Planning Group formed as a decision making, multi-agency body to consider pupils' whose Pastoral Support Programmes, IEPs, are not working. Pupils may also be disengaged, excluded or require alternative provision.

SCHOOL BASED EDUCATION
Positive outcome:
School based PSP; Re-integration; School based with time limited Support; School monitoring; Discipline Committee

LEA BASED EDUCATION & SUPPORT
Engaged:
Behaviour Support; ESW Service; Educational Psych.;
Disengaged
Home Tuition
Connexions
Education outside

ADDITIONAL EDUCATION SECTION
Disengaged:
Support in School Specialist Support Special School; Out of County

At all steps, the aim is to return pupils to mainstream education

Appendix 2: A proposed whole-school behaviour policy

BEHAVIOURAL MISSION

- Whole school community working towards mutual respect as a platform for learning

PROTOCOLS
(OUR SCHOOL'S WORKING PRACTICES)

- Working relationships based upon a Platform of Mutual Respect
- Rights, responsibility, rule-making with pupils
- Maintaining dignity and developing self-esteem
- Employment of non-confrontational stepped positive approach: take-up time, 'four to one', mediation, TIBing
- Corporate planning for behaviour ownership with known consequences, rewards and sanctions: Compliance = Opportunity
- Constantly, Communicate, Clearly with Consistency Conviction and Care
- 'Where pupils are at': conduct, emotions and learning behaviours

CLASSROOM PLAN

- Clear classroom rules
- Known consequences
- Differentiated curriculum
- Taught preferred practices
- Least intrusive to most intrusive interventions
- Positive reinforcement plan
- Planning for entrance, exit and constructive time out
- Behaviour ownership
- Empathy

SCHOOL-WIDE PLAN

- Corridor supervision
- Playground supervision
- Cover lessons
- Lunch times
- After-school activities
- Wet break times
- Out-of-school:
  trips
  sports
  swimming
- Anti-bullying
- Drugs and alcohol
- Child protection

CONSEQUENCES

- Whole-school planning for the 'What ifs'
- ABC
- Home–school agreement
- Individual and group planning
- Responding to legislation
- What help is out there?

'Rubber Boundary'
- Pastoral Support Programmes
- IEPs
- Behaviour Audit

171

References

Bernard, M. E. (1987), *Staying Rational in an Irrational World: Albert Ellis and Rational-emotive Therapy.* Melbourne, Australia: McCulloch-Macmillan.

Bernard, M. E., Joyce, M. R. and Rosewarne, P. M. (1983), 'Helping teachers cope with stress: a rational-emotive approach.' In A. Ellis and M. E. Bemard (eds), *Rational-emotive Approaches to the Problems of Childhood.* New York: Pelum Press, pp. 415–67.

Berne, E. (1976), *Games People Play: The Psychology of Human Relationships.* Harmondsworth: Penguin Psychology and Psychiatry.

Bible Societies (1994), New Life Good News Bible, Paul's Second Letter to the Corinthians, Ch. 2, V. 7. London: HarperCollins.

Bloom, B. S. (1976), *Human Characteristics and School Learning.* Maidenhead: McGraw-Hill.

Bower, E. M. (1969), *Early Identification of Emotionally Handicapped Children in School.* Springville, IL.: Charles C. Thomas.

Bray, M. (1997), 'Poppies on the Rubbish Heap.' In *Sexual Abuse: The Child's Voice.* London: Jessica Kingsley, p. 45.

Charlton, T. and David, K. (eds) (1993), *Managing Misbehaviour in Schools* (2nd edn). London: Routledge.

Chisholm, B., Kearney, D., Knight, H., Little, H., Morris, S. and Tweddle, D. (1986), *Preventive Approaches to Disruption (PAD).* Basingstoke: Macmillan.

References

Colby, D. and Harper, T. (1985), *Preventing Classroom Disruption*. London: Croom Helm.

Cole, T., Visser, J. and Upton, G. (1998), *Effective Schooling for Pupils with Emotional and Behavioural Difficulties*. London: David Fulton.

Coleman, J. C. and Hendry, L. (1990), *The Nature of Adolescence* (2nd edn). London: Routledge.

Cooper, P. and Upton, G. (1990), 'An ecosystemic approach to emotional and behavioural difficulties in schools.' *Educational Psychology*, 10 (4): 301–21.

Cowley S. (2006), *Getting the Buggers to Behave* (3rd edn). London: Continuum.

Davie, R. (1993), 'Assessing and understanding children's behaviour'. In T. Charlton and K. David (eds), *Managing Misbehaviour in Schools* (2nd edn). London: Routledge.

Daniels, H., Visser, J., Cole, T. and de Reybekill, N. (1998), *Emotional and Behavioural Difficulties in Mainstream Schools*. DfEE Research Report No 90. London: HMSO.

Department for Education (DfE) (1993), *Pupils with Problems: Draft Guidance Circulars*. London: DfE.

Department for Education (DfE) (1994), 'Pupil behaviour and discipline.' In *Pupils with Problems, Circular 8/94*. London: DfE, para 20, p. 11. (Section Title: Whole-school Behaviour Policies and Approaches.)

Department for Education and Employment (DfEE) (1999), *Draft Guidance, Social Inclusion: Pupil Support*. London: HMSO.

Department of Education and Science (DES) (1978), *Special Educational Needs (The Warnock Report)*. London: HMSO.

Department of Education and Science (DES) (1981), *Education Act (/98/)*, *Special Education*. London HMSO.

Department of Education and Science (DES) (1986), *Education (No. 2), Act/986*. London: HMSO.

Department of Education and Science (DES) (1989), Circular 22/89/ Welsh Office Circular 54/89, *Assessments and Statement of Special Educational Needs: Procedures within the*

Education, Health and Social Services (Annex to HN98920/ HN (FP), 19/LASSL (89)7WOC54/89). London: HMSO.

Department for Education and Skills (DfES) (2003), *Key Stage 3 National Strategy: Key messages: Behaviour and attendance strand*. Ref DfES 0391/2003. London: HMSO. www.dfes. gov.uk

Department for Education and Skills (DfES) (2004a), *Key Stage 3 National Strategy 2004–5*. Ref DfES 0122-2004G. London: HMSO.

Department for Education and Skills (DfES) (2004b), *Key Stage 3 National Strategy: Behaviour & Attendance Training Materials: Core Day 2 – Developing effective practice across the school*. Ref DfES 0055-2004. London: HMSO.

Dreikurs, R., Grunwald, B. and Pepper, F. (1982), *Maintaining Sanity in the Classroom*. New York: Harper and Row.

Education Act 1993. London: HMSO.

Education Act 1996. London: HMSO.

Education Act Supplement 1997. London: HMSO.

Education Reform Act 1998. London: HMSO.

Egan, G. (1998), *The Skilled Helper* (6th edn). Pacific Grove, California: Brooks/Cole Publishing Company.

Elton Report (1989), *Discipline in Schools*. Report by the Committee of Enquiry chaired by Lord Elton. London: HMSO

Farrell, P. (1995), 'Guidelines for helping children with emotional and behavioural difficulties.' In P. Farrell (ed.), *Children with Emotional and Behavioural Difficulties*. London: Falmer Press, p. 105.

Galloway, D. and Goodwin, C. (1987), *The Education of Disturbing Children*. Harlow: Longman.

Glasser, W. (1986), *Control Theory in the Classroom*. New York: Harper and Row.

Golman, D. (1996), *Emotional Intelligence*. London: Bloomsbury.

Gray, P., Miller, A. and Noakes, J. (1994), *Challenging Behaviour in Schools*. London and New York: Routledge.

Greenhalgh, P. (1994), *Emotional Growth and Learning*. London: Routledge.

Gribble, G. W. (1989), *Behavioural Support in a High School*. Unpublished M.Ed. Thesis, School of Education, University College of North Wales, Bangor.

Gribble, G. W. (1993a), 'Keeping our heads above water.' *Special Children*, October 1993, 14–18.

Gribble, G. W. (1993b), *Behaviour Management for Teachers: A Positive Approach to Discipline in Schools*. Bangor, Wales: School of Education, University of Wales.

Hargreaves, D. H. (1972), *Interpersonal Relationships in Education*. London: Routledge, Kegan and Paul.

Harris, T. (1973), *Winners and Losers*. Jacksonville, IL.: Argus Communications.

HMSO (1989), Discipline in Schools. Report by the Committee of Enquiry chaired by Elton. London: HMSO.

Hook, P. and Vass, A. (2002), *Confident Classroom Leadership*. London: David Fulton.

Howell, K. (1998), 'Variables which influence student achievement.' In B. Rogers (ed.), *Behaviour Recovery* (2nd edn). Harlow: Longman.

Kolvin, I. (1981), *Help Starts Here*. London: Tavistock.

Kounin, J. S. (1977), *Discipline and Group Management in Classrooms*. New York: Holt, Rinehart and Winston.

Laing, R. D. (1970), *Knots*. Harmondsworth: Penguin Psychology and Psychiatry.

McGuiness, J. (1993), *Teachers, Pupils and Behaviour: A Managerial Approach*. London: Cassell.

McNamara, S. and Moreton, G. (1996), *Challenging Behaviour: Teaching Children with Emotional and Behavioural Difficulties in Primary and Secondary Classrooms*. London: David Fulton.

Maslow, A. H. (1954), *Motivation and Personality* (2nd edn). New York: Harper Row

Masson, J. (1990), *The Children Act 1989*. Text and commentary. London: Sweet and Maxwell.

Michel, Deborah (ed.) (1998), *The Behaviour Curriculum: A whole school approach to teaching positive behaviour and emotional competence in the Primary School.* Cumbria County Council: Cumbria Education Services. Tel.: 01228 606824.

Michel, Deborah (ed.) (2002), *The Positive Behaviour Curriculum: A Whole School Approach to Teaching Positive Behaviour and Emotional Competence in the Secondary School.* Cumbria County Council: Cumbria Education Services. Tel.: 01228 606824.

Mosley, J. (1999), *More Quality Circle Time.* Cambs: LDA.

Ofsted (2005), *Managing Challenging Behaviour: Better Education and Care.* Document Reference No. HMI 2363. www.ofsted.gov.uk

Olsen, J. and Cooper, P. (2001), *Dealing with Disruptive Students in the Classroom.* London: Routledge.

Parsons, C. (1996), *Final Report on Follow-up Survey of Permanent Exclusion from Schools in England, 1995/96.* Canterbury: Christ Church College.

Parsons, C. and Howlett, K. (1996), 'Permanent exclusion from school: a case where society is failing its children.' *Support for Learning,* 11 (3), 109–12.

Pearce, J. (1989), *Bad Behaviour: How to Deal with Naughtiness and Disobedience and Still Show you Love and Care for your Child.* London: Thorsons Publishing Group.

Postman, N. and Weingartner, C. (1976), *Teaching as a Subversive Activity.* Harmondsworth: Penguin Education Specials.

QCA/DfEE (1999), *Supporting the Target Setting Process: Guidance for Effective Target Setting for Pupils with Special Educational Needs.* London: DfEE.

QCA/DfES (2001), *Supporting School Improvement: Emotional and Behavioural Development.* London: QCA. www.qca.org.uk/6041.html

Rayner, S. (1998), 'Educating pupils with emotional and behaviour difficulties: pedagogy is the key!' *Emotional and Behavioural Difficulties*, 3 (2), Summer: 39–47.

Redl, F. and Wineman, D. (1952), *Controls from Within: Techniques for the Aggressive Child*. NY: Free Press.

Reid, K. (1986), *Disaffection from School*. London: Methuen.

Reid, K. (2000), *Tackling Truancy in Schools: A Practical Manual for Primary and Secondary Schools*. London: Methuen. ISBN 0415205085.

Riding, R. and Rayner, S. (1998), *Cognitive Styles and Learning Strategies*. London: David Fulton.

Robertson, J. (1990), *Effective Classroom Control*. London: Hodder and Stoughton (Educational).

Roffey, S. and O'Reirdan, T. (2001), *Young Children and Classroom Behaviour: Needs, Perspectives and Strategies*. London: David Fulton.

Rogers, B. (1989), *Decisive Discipline: Every Move You Make, Every Step You Take (A video learning package)*. Geelong, Victoria, Australia: The Institute of Educational Administration.

Rogers, B. (1990), *You Know the Fair Rule*. Victoria, Australia: Australian Council for Educational Research.

Rogers, B. (1994), *The Language of Discipline*. Plymouth: Northcote House.

Rogers, B. (1995), *Behaviour Management: A whole-school approach*. Melbourne, Australia: Ashton Scholastic.

Rogers, B. (1996), *Managing Teacher Stress*. London: Pitman Publishing.

Rogers, B. (1998), *Behaviour Recovery*. Harlow: Longman.

Rogers, B. (2002), *I Get By with a Little Help: Colleague Support in Schools*. Australia: Australian Council for Educational Research.

Rogers, C. T. R. (1980), *A Way of Being*. Boston: Houghton Mifflin.

Rogers, J. (1985), *The Dictionary of Clichés*. New York: Ballantine Books.

Rutter, M., Maughan, B., Mortimore, P. and Ouston, J. (1979), *Fifteen Thousand Hours*. London: Open Books.

Smith, C. and Laslett, R. (1993), *Effective Classroom Management: A Teacher's Guide*. London: Routledge

Spalding, B. (2000), 'Quiet Places'. In *British Journal of Special Education*, 27 (3), September, 129–34.

Topping, K. (1983), *Educational Systems for Disruptive Adolescents*. London: Croom Helm.

Trowell, J. and Bower, M. (1995), *The Emotional Needs of Children and Their Families: Using Psychoanalytic Ideas in the Community*. London: Routledge, pp. 38–53.

Visser, J. and Rayner, S. (eds) (1999), *Emotional and Behavioural Difficulties: A Course Reader*. Lichfield, UK: QEd.

Webb, S. (1992), 'Helping Troublesome Children'. *Croner's Head Teachers' Bulletin*, November, 3–4.

Welsh Office (1999), *Shaping the Future for Special Education – An Action Programme for Wales: The BEST Programme, Building Excellent Schools Together*. Cardiff: The Welsh Office.

Wheldall, K. and Merrett, F. (1984), *Positive Teaching: The Behavioural Approach*. London: Unwin Education Books.

Whitney, B. (1993), *The Children Act and Schools*. London: Kogan Page.

Wilson, M. and Evans, M. (1980), 'Education of Disturbed Pupils'. *Schools Council Working Paper 65*. London: Methuen.

Wolfendale, D. (1992), *Empowering Parents and Teachers: Working for Children*. London: Cassell.

Wragg, E. C. (1993), *Class Management*. London: Routledge.

in a class of your own ...

'Bill knows schools and students. He is clearly sensitive to the stresses we all face in our profession day-to-day. [Bill deals] with a wide range of issues with candour, sensitivity and good humour.' DR BILL ROGERS

A pacey and enjoyable guide for teachers designed to help them improve their behaviour management skills. Emphasizing the need to maintain a positive approach – even when things get REALLY tough – Bill Gribble writes in a down-to-earth and realistic way. This book should prove invaluable for all teachers.

A teacher for many years, BILL GRIBBLE is now an expert on behaviour management and runs regular INSET days on managing behaviour.

WITH A FOREWORD BY BILL ROGERS

continuum

Photography by Mike Inns

ISBN 0-8264-8553-7

9 780826 485533